JEWISH
FOLK TALES

JEWISH FOLK TALES

by Leo Pavlát

illustrated by
Jiří Běhounek

translated by
Stephen Finn

Greenwich House
New York

First published in Great Britain 1986
by Beehive Books, an imprint of
Orbis Book Publishing Corporation Ltd., London
A BPCC plc company
Translated by Stephen Finn
Graphic design by Aleš Krejča
© Artia, Prague 1986

1986 edition published by Greenwich House,
distributed by Crown Publishers, Inc.

Printed in Czechoslovakia by Polygrafia, Prague

ISBN 0–517–602148

h g f e d c b a

Contents

Contents

The Glow
of the Hanukkiya

All Jewish holidays are beautiful because of what they recall and beautiful in their customs. There are special rituals, a solemn service in the synagogue, hymns written just for the occasion, foods not served at other times. Jewish children enjoy these times spent with their elders, feast after feast and year after year. But if you were to ask them which holiday they looked forward to most, they would probably say 'Hanukka!'

Hanukka — the feast of lights. Many, many centuries ago, the powerful King of Syria, Antiochus Epiphanes, tried to make the Jews renounce their faith. He forbade them to worship the one God or to read and study the holy books. They were not allowed to observe their holidays or to abide by the laws of their fathers. Antiochus was a cruel king, and his army was strong. If any of the Jews dared disobey his orders, he had them put to death. Even the temple at Jerusalem was shamelessly desecrated. The Jews were distressed. What were they to do? Where were they to turn? Some took to the hills to live according to their religion, but even there they were never safe from the king's soldiers. Then the high priest Mattathias Maccabee and his five sons joined the fugitives and persuaded the Jews to make a stand against the Syrians. Mattathias' eldest son, Judah, gathered together a small army, and three years to the day after Antiochus had issued his decree the Jews fought a victorious battle against great odds. The Maccabees entered the ransacked temple and threw out the pagan idols; then they prepared it for reconsecration. At last all was ready except for the lighting of the temple lamp with its seven branches. But for this they needed specially consecrated olive oil, of which they could find only one jar. It was not enough, for the lamp must never be extinguished, and the oil from one jar was only enough for one day. But the Jews lit the lamp just the same. In its light they prayed to God, giving thanks that they were again free. Then a miracle took place. The lamp, filled with the oil from one small jar, burned not one day, but two, three, and in the end a whole eight days — long enough for the priests to prepare new oil.

It is in memory of this that the Jews keep the feast of lights, Hanukka. The holiday is especially dear to children. They get presents, and eat potato cakes called latkes and doughnuts called savganiyot. But most of all they look forward to lighting the candles. On the first day they light one, on the next day two, and so on until on the eighth day the hanukkiya, *the eight-branched lamp, is all lit up.*

Hanukka begins in the middle of winter, on the twenty-fifth day of the month of Kislev, according to the Jewish calendar. This is the time when the days are shortest and the nights longest — the time for legends and tales to be told. The best known of these, and some which are less known, are contained in this book, which is divided into eight lights, like the hanukkiya. Each light contains stories from a different time and a different land, since the Jews have for thousands of years been dispersed among the other nations; they still are, though many of them are again able to live in the land of their fathers, Israel. Each of the lights has a few fables added to it for good measure. Their brevity clearly shows up two characteristics of all Jewish tales: the celebration of wisdom and piety, and the use of wit to provoke thought.

The lights of the hanukkiya are lit using a special candle called a shammess. *This Hebrew word is the name of the attendant in the synagogue — he who serves and assists. The eight lights in this book also have their 'shammess', the tale called 'The End of the World'. It is a reminder that people cannot get by without human charity. Without it, without love for mankind, not even the flame of wisdom and wit would ever burn properly.*

✡

THE FIRST
LIGHT

The Creation of the World and Abraham and Moses, Fathers of the Jewish Nation

Why the Jews Have a Peculiar Calendar

A long time ago there was nothing anywhere. Only a great emptiness stretched out on all sides, without beginning or end, and it was ruled over by God. There was no seeing or hearing the emptiness, and it could neither be grasped nor felt; but when God decided to create the world, everything changed. All at once there was something to look at, and God surveyed His work carefully. But the first world was not to His liking, so He destroyed it and made some others. None of them suited Him either, so He got rid of them, too. In the end God stretched out His right hand and made the Heavens. Then He put out His left hand and made the Earth. That was the start of the best of all worlds that have ever been created, and that is the one that we live in.

But at first the Earth was dark, and quite barren, covered only with stark mountains and deep seas. "Dear God ," it sighed, "I am all alone. You have kept the Heavens close to you, but I have been banished, left here with only hard stones and cold water for company, far away from You!"

God bent down towards the Earth. "I had no wish to wrong you," He said, "and I know how to help you. Soon grass, flowers and trees will spring up on you; many plants will grow from your soil. You will be filled with pleasant fragrances, and your fruits will nourish man and beast. You will be their home, and will delight in their voices and the laughter of their children."

At these words the Earth was content, and God made the Sun and the Moon. The moment they lit up in the Heavens, the darkness was gone, and the world was filled with light. The Sun and the Moon were the same size. They had the same brightness, and they each shone for the same length of time. God had given them equal power and equal rights. The two heavenly bodies took turns to light up the sky, and time on Earth was measured according to their rising and setting.

But the Moon was not satisfied. "Why should the Sun have as much light as I ?" it said to itself. "I shall go and complain, the way the Earth did. If God heard its plea, He will hear mine, too. After all God is the King of Kings; He should know better than anyone that no two rulers can share the same crown."

So the Moon came before God's throne and said, "God, it isn't right that You have granted me and the Sun the same size and the same amount of light. How are people to tell which of us is which?"

"Would you like to shine more brightly?" asked God.

"There is no need for that," replied the Moon. "When I rise, everyone is getting ready for bed, and the few wandering souls who have no roof above their heads don't need more light. It would be better if You were to take away a little of the Sun's brightness. What do men need all that light for?"

God grew sad. "I wanted there to be peace and quiet for everyone," He thought, "and here is envy already. If I leave it unpunished, it will destroy the most beautiful of the worlds I have created." He gazed at the Moon sadly, and said, "Moon, you are right. If that is how you feel, then you and the Sun cannot be equal. So I am going to turn part of you into hundreds of thousands of stars, and you can share your brightness with them. Because you envied the Sun its light, you shall in future receive yours from it. And since you thought that I should grant your unjust wish as I granted the just wish of the Earth, you will always be in its shade when it is passing you!"

God had no sooner spoken these words, than the Moon began to grow smaller and its light became dimmer. Stars appeared throughout the Heavens, and the glory of the Moon dissolved in their shimmering glow. All that remained was the dull reflection of the Sun's brightness, and the shadow thrown by the Earth.

The Moon began to cry. "Dear God," it begged, "forgive my vanity. Take pity on me!"

"I cannot take back my word," said God. "But I will grant you one comfort. The stars you have given your light to will never desert you. They will accompany you and glorify you. Not only that, but the Jews will number their days, weeks and years by you, and count the beginning of their days by the stars. Thus men will never forget that envy can darken the brightest of lights."

Since then the stars have accompanied the Moon, and the Jews have arranged their calendar by it. They do not even begin to count the hours of the day from the sunrise, like other nations, but from the appearance of the first three stars. And when the Moon's crescent begins to grow larger, they say a special prayer in its light. That is when the Moon is happiest. The full moon is approaching, when it will not be in the shadow of the Earth, and when it hears the Creator praised, it forgets its sin of long ago.

The Angel
Shemchazay

When the Earth was first peopled, there were born on it such beautiful girls that even the angels crowded to first one end of the skies, then the other, gazing in wonder at the enchanting daughters of man. The angels wanted more than anything to get close to them. The girls, as if they knew, grew ever more pleasing.

One day the angels Azael and Shemchazay made a plan. "Let us descend from Heaven, and go to live among the daughters of man," they said. "With their beauty and our heavenly power the Earth will be a better place. We shall bring into the world children with whom no creature can compare."

So they called together their companions and told them their plan. Some of the angels disagreed. "It is not fitting for us to love such lowly creatures," they said. But others were delighted. In the end two hundred angels decided they would leave Heaven for the daughters of man. God Himself tried in vain to dissuade them, warned them in vain that angels cannot live with men, and that their children would bring misfortune to Earth. Infatuated by the beauty of the daughters of man, the angels swore that they would take them as wives, and descended to the peak of Mount Hermon, whence they could see to the furthest corners of the Earth. They took a good look at all the lands in the world, and there was not a nook, nor a cranny, nor a human being that escaped their gaze. Each of them chose the girl that most took his fancy, and the girls, flattered to have attracted the attentions of angels, were only too willing to become their brides.

The angels built for their wives new houses which were tall and strong, such as had never been seen on Earth before. They showed the earthlings how to till the soil and tend their trees, and brought from the meadows fragrant herbs to teach the art of healing. To help men in their work they gave them new tools, and revealed to them how fire can be put to good use. The angels taught people to read and write and draw pictures, to work with a potter's wheel and to model objects out of clay. Men began to trade, and traveled from place to place, so that they got to know other lands and other customs. Soon people became so accomplished in their new skills that the whole Earth began to flourish.

The most beautiful of all the angels' brides was the wife of Shemchazay. Her name was Ishtar, and Shemchazay loved her more dearly than any man could love another creature. Whether Ishtar was working in the fields, washing by the riverside, or cooking the family's supper, Shemchazay would follow her with his eyes. Ishtar's house was the finest in the whole land. Shemchazay filled it with splendors whose beauty the works of man could never match, and was all the time bringing home new bowls, decorated cushions, curtains and carpets, which he hoped would please his wife. But Shemchazay's gifts brought no joy to Ishtar. She remained downcast, as if troubled by some oppressive secret, and the more the angel tried to raise her spirits, the gloomier she grew. After this had gone on for some months, Shemchazay could bear it no longer.

"Ishtar," he said, "you are so beautiful, and yet so sad. Tell me the cause of your pain. I vow I shall do whatever you ask, if only it will make you happy."

"Will you truly do whatever I ask?" Ishtar asked him, in a voice that was little more than a whisper.

"Indeed I will!" cried Shemchazay. "Speak, Ishtar: tell me what to do."

Then Ishtar fixed the angel with her great, dark eyes, and said, "All right, I'll tell you. Just as you, an angel, wished to live here on Earth with a daughter of man, I, a human being, long to live in Heaven, close to God. If you are indeed going to keep your promise, then tell me the ineffable name of God."

Now Shemchazay was sorry he had made his hasty promise, and begged his wife to change her request. Was not the knowledge and use of God's ineffable name the privilege of the chosen few? But Ishtar insisted, and in the end Shemchazay, with a heavy heart, whispered to her that which had never before been revealed to a mortal.

The moment Ishtar heard the tremendous word, she ran out onto the flat roof of the house. Lifting her arms up to Heaven, she threw back her head, and addressed God in the manner of the creatures of Heaven. At that instant she began to tremble, and her body shone more brightly than the purest gold. God had heard Ishtar's plea and, touched by the love she felt for Him, He raised this daughter of man up to Heaven, where He made her a bright star.

What misfortune had befallen Shemchazay! His dear Ishtar had ascended to God, while he, a heavenly one, remained on Earth. There was no bodily torment that could equal the suffering of his soul. He reproved himself for his rash promise, then sadly stroked the gifts he had showered upon Ishtar; he did not know what to do or where to turn. He wept for whole days and nights, but, lament as he might, no one could return his wife to him.

Shortly after Ishtar's disappearance, the wives of the other angels gave birth to children. The news spread through all the lands of the Earth, and the people rejoiced and made merry. Great feasts were held in the children's honor, lasting many days; but before the last of the wine was drunk, joy gave way to horror. Instead of splendid creatures, superior to men, the infants grew before people's very eyes into giants. In no time at all they were three thousand feet tall, and they soon began to destroy everything. They devoured the crops that men had worked so hard to produce and the fruit of the trees, so that men began to go hungry. Then the giants seized the livestock. Every day each of them ate a thousand camels, a thousand horses and a thousand cattle, and when all these were gone they slew the birds and beasts of the forests, the snakes of the mountainside, and the fish of the rivers and seas. Then they started to eat men. Terrified, people took to the rocks and

hid in caves and holes dug deep in the ground. The giants continued their rampage, now devouring one another; their fearful struggles laid waste the desolate forests, fields and gardens more surely than the fiercest tempest.

A fit of destruction seized the beings of the Earth. The angels were no match for their gigantic sons, and fled before them as men did. Some of them even joined forces with the giants and spread evil. Azael, once Shemchazay's closest friend, began to teach men to forge swords, spears, shields and armor. The women he led astray with gaily-colored clothes, precious metals and gems. He showed them how to make gleaming bracelets and beaten rings, offered them inlaid needles for their hair. Soon the women had no time for anything but making themselves fancy, while the men went to war with their newly acquired weapons. Nation slew nation without quarter, while the bodies of both dead and living fell prey to the ever-present giants.

By now many of the angels regretted that they had not listened to their companions. They wished they had never fallen for the charms of the daughters of man, rebuked themselves for not heeding God's warning. The most mournful of all was Shemchazay. Without Ishtar life on Earth brought him no joy anyway, and when he saw the Earth infested with giants and human evil his grief was sharpened. Shemchazay's suffering grew greater day by day, and finally, when it reached up to Heaven itself, God took pity on him. He raised the angel once again to the heights of Heaven, closer to Ishtar, and there Shemchazay hung his head earthwards. Thus he was always looking down on the devastation the coming of the angels had brought, and seeing the punishment God had inflicted on the Earth: the waves of a flood buried all evil beneath them. But Shemchazay remained half way between Earth and Heaven, where his penitence continues to this day.

How Abraham Came to Know God

Abraham is the father of the Jewish nation. By the time he was born, many years had passed since the Flood, but men had not improved their ways much. They dabbled in magic, worshipped the stars and even different animals, but to their Creator, the one true God, they gave not a thought.

While Abraham was still a small boy, he lived with his father Terach in a cave. Here Terach wished to hide the child from the cruel King Nimrod, for the magi had told Nimrod that the Jews who would be descendants of Abraham would one day swallow up his kingdom. So Nimrod decided to kill the boy. For many a long year Abraham was not to see the light of day, and when he first set eyes on the sun, he called out in wonder: "So much light can come only from him who rules the whole world!" And Abraham bowed down before the might of the sun; but then the sun set, and its place in the heavens was taken by the moon and the stars.

"I was wrong," said Abraham to himself. "This light is surely mightier than the first. It is smaller than the other, but it is attended by thousands of servants." So Abraham lifted up his hands to heaven and invoked the moon. But when daybreak came the moon disappeared and the sun took its place.

"This is a strange thing," thought Abraham to himself. "That such great lights should have to take turns in the sky. They would scarcely leave the heavens of their own accord; they must obey some invisible being more mighty than themselves. He is sure to be the ruler of the whole world, a lordly and powerful ruler, who cannot be seen, but whom none can surpass!"

Thus it was that Abraham came to know God; but he told no one of his thoughts. He had to be cautious in front of his own father, Terach, in particular, for Terach saw things quite differently. He worshipped idols, offered sacrifices to them, and even made them out of clay. He would make them just as people wanted them, and he hoped that one day his son would carry on his work. But God had other plans.

One day, Terach set off on a journey of several days. He put his whole house in Abraham's charge, telling him the price of each of the idols, and saying that he should sell as many as he could.

Before long a man came knocking at the door. "What do you want?" Abraham asked him.

"My wife sent me to buy some sort of a god. One that will watch over us and will not require too many sacrifices."

Abraham nodded his head. "Tell me, how old are you?"

"Sixty years," the man replied.

"You are sixty years old?" said Abraham, laughing. "And you would adore an idol which is just one day old?"

The man was ashamed, and went away empty-handed.

The next day a woman entered Terach's house, carrying a bowl of flour. "Take this flour, please," she said to Abraham, "and offer it up to one of the gods."

"What nonsense is this?" cried Abraham. "Is a piece of clay able to eat?" He took up a stick, and out of anger at man's stupidity smashed all the idols to smithereens. He left only the largest of the figures in one piece, and placed the stick in its hand and the bowl of flour at its feet.

When Terach returned home and came upon this scene of destruction, he yelled: "What is the meaning of this?"

"Do not be angry, father," Abraham replied, "for a strange thing has happened. Some days ago a woman brought a bowl of flour as an offering to the gods. But as soon as they saw it, they began to quarrel. They all began to shout at once that they wanted to eat first, until the biggest of them took a stick and broke all the others to pieces. But as you can see, he did not eat the flour; if you wish, father, I shall ask your god if he is hungry yet."

No sooner had Terach heard his son's words, than he began to shout: "What is this you say? How could statues which I made with my own hands be hungry, or break each other?"

"You see, father," laughed Abraham, "you yourself have said it. Your idols have eyes, but they do not see. They have ears, but they cannot hear. Their noses can't smell, their mouths can't speak, their hands don't touch, their feet don't walk. They are not even the equals of man; they are only lumps of lifeless clay — and you would worship them as gods?"

Terach did not reply. Abraham went outside in a merry mood, and from then on he made no secret to his father of his knowledge of the one true God.

Eliezer
in Sodom and Gomorrah

When Abraham took a wife, he brought into his house a young man called Eliezer, who was one of the most honorable and truthful men in the world. He served Abraham and his wife Sarah for many years, and never thought of anything but his master's good.

One day, Abraham heard that in the nearby towns of Sodom and Gomorrah there lived extraordinarily wicked and godless folk. He could hardly believe the stories he heard about these places. There were, it was said, four judges who ruled these towns — Liar, Dishonorable, Deceiver and Lawbender. When someone cut an ear off his neighbor's ass, they decided that he should keep the ass until the ear grew again. Whoever had one ox had to be public herder for one day, and whoever had none had to do the job for two days. There was a bridge across a stream which ran close to Sodom, where strangers had to pay a toll. The toll was four gold pieces, but if anyone chose to wade across the stream instead, he had to pay twice as much. Guests were unwelcome in Sodom and Gomorrah, and beggars were given a gold coin instead of bread. But the coin was marked, so that it was impossible for the beggar to spend it, and when he died of hunger the money was returned to his benefactor.

The thought of these things kept Abraham awake at night, and one day he sent Eliezer to find out if the stories were true. First of all Eliezer went to Sodom. It was late in the afternoon when he arrived, so he went straight to an inn to seek a bed for the night. First he looked in through the window, and what did he see? In the middle of the room there were two beds, each with a guest tied to it. One of them was too long for his bed, and the innkeeper was just about to put this right by cutting off his feet. The second traveler was shorter than his bed, and two men were stretching him out to make him fit. But since Eliezer had the shoulders of an ox and hands like shovels, he had little to fear, and stepped boldly into the inn. The innkeeper pretended he was delighted to see him, and at once offered him a bed to lie in. But Eliezer would not go anywhere near it, explaining that he had once vowed to sleep only on the floor, and before the inkeeper and his accomplices could do anything about it he had stretched himself out on the ground.

The innkeeper shook with anger, but he had no wish to pit his strength against Eliezer's. But early the next morning, he went out and stirred up the menfolk of Sodom. Then he woke Eliezer up and pushed him out of the door. A crowd of people thronged the street in front of the inn. Immediately they began to abuse Eliezer, pelting him with mud and stones. Eliezer simply smiled; then he was struck a sharp blow on the head with a stone, and he started to bleed. The crowd fell silent, and one of the town's judges stepped forward, accompanied by the man who had wounded Eliezer.

The judge said to Eliezer, "I see that this good fellow has saved you the sum of five gold pieces, since that is the fee you would pay a physician for letting your blood. Pay your debt at once!"

Eliezer lost his temper. "So that is how you do things here! Very well, then; what is sauce for the goose is sauce for the gander!" And he took up a stone, hurled it at the judge, and then said, "It seems to me, your honor, that you, too, are bleeding. But if you would be so kind as to pay my fee to this fellow who wounded me, then both our debts will be settled!"

And without more ado, Eliezer took to his heels. Leaving Sodom, he entered Gomorrah. It was some days now since he had left Abraham's house, and he was famished. But no one would sell him any food, and in Gomorrah hospitality was the greatest sin of all. To invite a stranger to one's table was punishable by death, so everyone drove Eliezer away from his door as if he were a disease instead of a fellow human being. At the end of his strength, Eliezer staggered up to a house where a wedding-feast was in progress. There were tables laden with food and drink; the guests were so full they couldn't eat another bite, but still new dishes were being brought all the time.

Eliezer was so hungry by now that he didn't bother to ask anyone's leave; he simply sat down in front of a platter of roast meat.

"Who invited you?" demanded his host angrily.

"Why, have you forgotten?" replied Eliezer, with a good-natured smile. "You did, of course."

The moment he heard this, Eliezer's neighbor took to his heels. He knew quite well that if anyone were to overhear, he might be sentenced to death for hospitality. Eliezer dealt with the next of his companions the same way, then with a third and a fourth, and so on until he found himself sitting at the richly spread table all by himself. He ate and drank his fill, and then took some food with him for the journey to give to any poor travelers he met.

Thus it was that Eliezer got the better of the malevolent citizens of Gomorrah too, and returned to Abraham's house with a light heart.

Moses Delivered

In ancient times, there were so few Jews that they all knew each other by name. Abraham and his wife Sarah had a son called Isaac, and Isaac's wife begat Jacob. Years passed by, the sun rose and set over and over again, until by and by Jacob's children, too, saw the light of day. These children gave rise to twelve great tribes. No longer did the children of Israel live under one roof; their tents were counted in dozens, and they numbered hundreds and thousands. But it was a time of tribulation for the Jewish people: they had no land of their own, and they had to settle in Egypt. Egypt was ruled by a mighty pharaoh, who hated the Jews. He forgot that they had once been invited to his land, that they had worked hard there for scores of years. He placed them in bondage, and even gave orders that their male offspring were to be thrown into the River Nile the moment they were born.

God saw the trials of His people, and resolved to send them a deliverer who would one day punish the cruel pharaoh and lead the Jews out of Egypt. He was a wondrous man, and his name was Moses.

When Moses was born, the room he was born in was filled with light, as if the sun had entered it. "What a beautiful boy!" cried his mother in delight.

"If only he might rid us of our troubles," his father sighed.

His parents turned to each other and were sad. According to the pharaoh's decree not a single Jewish boy was to be spared. How could Moses help his people?

The boy's father and mother pondered over what they might do, and suddenly they had an idea. They would throw the child into the Nile, as the pharaoh had ordered, but in a caulked wicker basket. "Perhaps someone will rescue him," said Moses' mother.

Right away the lad's father wove a fine, sound basket, and tarred it well. Then he laid his son carefully in the bottom and sent the basket floating down the Nile. It floated for many hours before getting caught up in the reeds by the bank. The weather was very hot that day, with not a cloud in the sky. God had ordered the sun to make the sand and the stones good and hot. Lots of people hurried down to the river to cool off, and it so happened that the pharaoh's daughter Batia went there, along with her servant-girls. The girls were giggling and playing, when the princess suddenly spied the basket containing little Moses.

"Look what I've found!" she called to her companions, and hurried towards the basket to pick the little boy up. But the servant-girls began to shout. "My lady, that is a Jewish boy! If you rescue him, you will be defying your father's orders!"

Before they could open their mouths to speak again they went flying into the water. That was the work of the invisible Angel Gabriel, captain of the heavenly hosts. God had sent him to look after Moses, and the angel had not left the boy's side for an instant. While the servant-girls, wet through, were struggling to climb back up the river bank, Gabriel gave Moses a pinch to make him cry, so as to arouse the princess's pity even more; but it was unnecessary. Batia was already stretching out her hand towards Moses, and she nearly fell into the river herself. But no matter how far she bent over, she could not quite reach the basket. At that moment something strange happened. Gabriel used his powers to make the princess's arm longer, so that she was able to take hold of the basket without any trouble.

Then another wondrous thing occurred: the moment Batia touched little Moses, she was cured of an unsightly rash which none of the physicians of Egypt had been able to rid her of.

Joyfully, Batia took hold of Moses and ran with him to the pharaoh's palace. When her father saw his daughter standing before him, healthy and beautiful, he agreed that she should keep the child. Moses was saved. Batia loved him like her own son. The child soon became the favorite of the pharaoh's subjects, too, and in the end the pharaoh himself would sometimes take the boy on his knee.

One day, when Moses was about three, the pharaoh was speaking to Batia and rocking the child on his knee. All of a sudden, Moses grabbed hold of the royal crown and put it on his own head. The pharaoh was horrified. Had not the magi said that one who would some day overthrow him and destroy the whole of Egypt was already living close by him? The Egyptian ruler immediately summoned his counselors to explain what Moses had done: was it no more than a child's idle play, or was it a bad omen?

All the pharaoh's counselors agreed that it was wiser to put the boy to death — all except one, that is. Jethro disagreed. "My lord," he said, "you will surely not allow yourself to be frightened by a child. It is an easy matter to put the boy's intentions to the test. We shall place before Moses two bowls, one containing sparkling jewels, the other glowing embers. If the child was really trying to deprive you of your crown, he will be attracted by the jewels, and deserves death. But if it was only a child's foolish whim, he will put his hand in the fire."

Pharaoh liked Jethro's suggestion, and before long all was ready for the trial. Servants brought in a bowl of precious stones and one filled with hot coals, and the whole court waited with bated breath to see what Moses would do.

Straight away Moses reached for the largest of the gems. Gabriel again took a hand. He knew that Moses must not give himself away, so he gave him a push. Moses' hand landed in the bowl of hot coals, and he gave a shriek of pain. Startled, he thrust his fingers into his mouth, only to burn his tongue on an ember which had stuck to his hand.

So it was that, with God's help, Moses' life was saved once again. But he never forgot his ordeal. From the day he thrust the burning ember into his mouth to the day he died, he stammered when he spoke.

Moses' Staff

Years had passed by since the day the pharaoh's daughter had fished Moses out of the River Nile. The boy had grown into a fine young man, and though he wore the robes of an Egyptian lord, he never forgot that he was a Jew. Moses knew how his people suffered under the yoke of slavery; he saw the grief of the Jewish mothers, deprived of their sons at birth.

One day the young Moses was out walking in front of the pharaoh's palace. Lost in melancholy thought, he wandered to and fro; then suddenly he heard a loud cry of pain. He looked up, and saw an Egyptian soldier cruelly flogging some Jewish slaves. Unable to bear such injustice, Moses hurled himself upon the soldier, and in his anger killed him. But what was he to do now? To return to the pharaoh would mean punishment by death, and there was no one in the whole of Egypt to whom Moses could turn. So he fled into the neighboring country, where he wandered through the mountains and hid in deep ravines, until finally he found refuge with Jethro the priest. It was the same Jethro who had saved the boy's life when he put the pharaoh's crown on his head.

Jethro was no ordinary man. He could read the stars, and knew people's innermost thoughts and nature's secrets. The Egyptian pharaoh had once heard tell of Jethro's powers, and had asked him to serve as his counselor, which Jethro did for some years. When Jethro was about to leave Egypt to return home, the pharaoh asked him what reward he desired for his service.

"I have before me a long journey," replied Jethro. "I should therefore ask of you the old staff which lies in the palace vaults, to help me on my way."

The pharaoh was surprised at Jethro's request, for he had expected him to ask for gold, or money; but in the end he was pleased to have hired the wise man's services for so little, and he readily agreed.

But the staff which Jethro took home with him was not of ordinary wood, and he knew full well that if he were to search pharaoh's palace from top to bottom he would find no greater treasure. For the staff was cut from the Tree of Knowledge in Paradise.

When Adam, the first man, was driven out of the Garden of Eden, he was given the staff by the Creator to alleviate his sorrow. The staff had miraculous powers — it relieved weariness, and with its assistance even the hardest work could be done quickly. From Adam the staff was passed on to the god-fearing Noah. He used it to measure the Ark in which he survived the Flood, and after him the staff belonged to Abraham, father of all the Jews. It then passed to his son Isaac, and to Isaac's son Jacob. Thanks to the miraculous staff, Jacob's son Joseph became steward of all Egypt, and the wonders he performed with its help brought prosperity to the whole empire. But when Joseph died, the pharaoh had the staff brought to him. In his hands it lost its miraculous powers, so the pharaoh, disappointed, threw it among the rubbish in the vaults of the palace, where it lay for many a long year, until Jethro took it away.

Jethro decided to plant the staff in his garden. He placed it on the ground so that he could dig a hole for it, but at that instant the staff put out deep roots of its own accord. That was strange enough, but what was even stranger was that as time went by neither leaves, nor

blossom, nor fruit grew on the staff. Thinking this was due to the poor quality of the soil, Jethro wanted to move the staff to another spot, but try as he would he could not pull it up, and in the end he had to leave it where it was.

Jethro had a daughter, whose beauty was the talk of all the men in the land. Her name was Zipporah, which means little bird. Not a day went by without some suitor or other visiting Jethro's house. Zipporah was wooed by young and old; they offered her riches or boasted of their strength, their power or their wisdom; but she would simply take them into her father's garden to the place where the staff grew out of the ground.

"Whoever pulls the staff from the ground shall have my hand in marriage," she would say.

For Zipporah was not only beautiful, but also wise. She had learnt many things from her father, and she knew the staff would obey only him whom God had chosen.

Moses, after taking refuge at Jethro's house, helped with the housework, and took the sheep to pasture. He saw how beautiful the magus's daughter was, and he soon fell in love not only with her face, her laughter and her grace, like the rest of the menfolk, but also with her sweet disposition. It was no wonder that the longer he stayed near her, the more he longed to make her his wife. But he did not dare go near the wondrous staff. Had he not seen the strongest in the land put to shame by it? So he only dreamed about Zipporah, and had no inkling that she liked him too. She sought him out more and more often, and even found herself growing anxious that one of her suitors might indeed draw the staff from the ground.

But Zipporah's fears were unnecessary. Hundreds of hands had already gripped the staff; some of the suitors had even returned several times over to try to fulfil her condition, but none had succeeded. The staff remained firmly stuck in the ground, as if the other end were hundreds of feet deep, and no one could budge it so much as an inch.

When Moses took the sheep to pasture, he set out early in the morning, and did not return till dusk. While ever new suitors presented themselves at Jethro's house, Moses gazed at the sheep as they grazed. He liked to look into the sheeps' soft, faithful eyes. In them he saw the same humility as in the eyes of Zipporah, and a certain nameless pain which reminded him of his brothers and sisters in Egyptian bondage. At such moments Moses forgot all else, and felt only the trials and the humiliation of his people; but try as he would, he could not think of a way to help them.

One day he was even sadder than usual. The thought of his people's fate and of the girl he longed for made him so sad that tears came to his eyes. Then suddenly, he heard a voice from Heaven: "Moses," God said to him, "grieve no more. Return to Jethro's house, and go into the garden. No one has yet pulled the staff out, but you can do it. Take the staff; it will help you to save the Jews."

Moses did at once as God had instructed him. Jethro looked on in amazement as Moses drove the flock home in the middle of the day, but Zipporah was even more surprised. She had just been thinking about him, and when she saw him stride straight towards the staff, her heart began to pound. Moses grasped the staff, and at that instant he saw the holy name of God carved on the end of it. The moment he spoke that name, the power which

had held the staff in the ground was dissolved. Moses drew out the staff as if it were a blade of grass, and raised it high above his head. It was only then that he saw Zipporah standing in front of him. Moses stepped towards her and embraced her, and within a few days a wedding feast was held in Jethro's house. It was attended by many guests, among them Moses' protector, the Angel Gabriel. Jethro rejoiced to see what a blessed husband his daughter had found, and Zipporah was so happy she couldn't take her eyes off Moses. He too was in a merry mood.

"God has given me Zipporah," he thought with satisfaction, "and the staff which won her for me will also bring back joy to my people."

And so it happened. In the hands of Moses the staff regained its miraculous powers, and not even the soldiers or the magi of the pharaoh could resist it. Thus Moses fulfilled the promise with which he came into the world: he delivered the Jews from bondage in Egypt, as was God's will. After that Moses lived with Zipporah for many years, and by and by they had two sons, called Gershom and Eliezer. But the miraculous staff did not pass to either of them after Moses' death, and no man has ever seen it since.

The Most Powerful
Weapons of All

At the end of the Sixth Day of Creation, God summoned all the animals to him. They gathered together, animals, birds, fish and reptiles, and all rejoiced to see how perfectly God had created them. Each of the creatures thanked God; only one sheep stood sadly in front of His throne.

"What is the matter?" the Creator asked it. "Why are you not happy like the other animals?"

"I should like to be as cheerful as they," replied the sheep. "But you have created me quite defenceless. How am I to preserve my life?"

"Do you want me to give you claws like those of the bear or the hawk?" God asked.

The sheep shook its head.

"Or sharp teeth, like the lion or the wolf?"

"No," said the sheep. "I should like to have weapons which would help me, but which would harm no one."

God considered these words of the sheep, and then said: "You want to live in peace and love; therefore I shall do as you ask. I shall give you qualities which will be a protection against evil."

And he made the sheep humble, faithful and patient.

Why the Crow Hops

When God created the crow, He not only gave him powerful wings, but strong legs as well, so that he could walk as well as he could fly. The crow was quite satisfied with his body, until one day he caught sight of a dove walking by, and from that moment his peace of mind was gone. "What a beautiful, graceful way of walking," he thought. "That is how a noble bird should walk — not with a heavy gait like mine."

The crow watched the dove carefully, and secretly tried to copy him. He stepped high and shook himself, until he felt elegant and dignified; but, suddenly, unused to walking about like that, he missed his step and broke his leg. How ashamed he was! All the other birds laughed at him, and in his mortification the crow longed to walk again as he had before. Finally, his leg was healed. The crow stood up and tried to take his first step, but alas, he had forgotten how to walk like a crow, and had never learnt to walk like a dove. So he began to hop along, and has done so ever since. Well, you know what they say: if you try to get too much, you are likely to lose what little you have.

THE SECOND LIGHT

King David and King Solomon

The Borrowed
Egg

David was a great Jewish king. When God created his soul, He imbued it with the song of birds and the gentle rustle of the wind in the leaves, tinged it with the purling of streams and the melody of those who lift up their prayers to God. David's heart was filled with songs, and when he grew up, he sang them in praise of the Creator. His singing was accompanied by the tune of the harp which hung over his bed, a harp whose strings were sounded at midnight by the breath of the northerly wind. But David's fame not only lay in his skill as a songster, for he was also a great soldier, and during his reign the Jews had a great empire.

One evening, when David's army was encamped in the field, they were given boiled eggs for supper. Among the soldiers was a young fellow from David's bodyguard who had eaten very little at midday, and therefore finished his meal before the others. The soldiers had scarcely settled down to their food when the young man turned to his neighbor and said: "Lend me one of your eggs, so that I may not sit here with an empty plate."

"Take one, by all means," the soldier replied, "but you must promise to return the egg when I ask for it, along with all the profits which have accrued to it."

Not taking too much notice of what the other had said, the young soldier gave his promise and quickly ate the egg.

The years passed by. David and his army marched from one place to another, until at last they were back in Jerusalem. The soldier remembered the old debt he was owed, and went to his comrade in David's bodyguard to ask for its repayment.

The debtor was taken aback to find that his creditor was asking for much more than the return of the original egg, but the other soldier reminded him of his promise.

"Then how much do I owe you?" asked the soldier from David's bodyguard.

"Count up with me," the other bade him. "From one egg in one year a chicken hatches and grows into a hen. In the next year the hen gives eighteen chickens, and the next year each of those has eighteen of its own. And so it goes. Come with me to the market-place. We shall ask the price of a hen, and then we can tot up your debt."

When the soldier from David's bodyguard realized the magnitude of his debt, he was furious. He said he hadn't so much money in the world, but his comrade insisted the debt be paid; so in the end the pair of them decided to take the matter before King David himself.

The two of them went before their ruler with the same hope of satisfaction, but when they returned only one was rejoicing. David had confirmed that it was not enough to return a single egg, and the unfortunate debtor did not know where to turn. He stopped in front of the palace gates, staring in front of him helplessly.

"What has happened to you?" asked a young voice.

The soldier turned and saw David's son Solomon sitting there. He told the lad his tale of woe, ending with the bitter words: "I ate a single egg, and now I have a debt I shall not be able to pay off to the end of my days."

"If you like," Solomon told the poor fellow, "I will give you some advice."

"What?" asked the soldier impatiently.

Solomon leaned towards him and quietly, so no one would hear, whispered a few words in the soldier's ear. The soldier smiled broadly, thanked Solomon and left the town without delay.

A little way out of Jerusalem there was a field which the royal soldiers walked past every day. This was the spot the debtor made for. He ploughed the field, cooked a potful of beans and, as the soldiers began to pass by, started to scatter them in the furrows.

The soldiers halted. "What are you doing?" one of them asked in surprise.

"Can't you see?" replied the soldier from David's bodyguard. "I am sowing boiled beans."

"You must be mad. Whoever heard of boiled beans sprouting?"

"And whoever heard of a chicken hatching from a boiled egg?"

The young debtor then told them his story, and he did the same the next day, and the next. All day long he scattered boiled beans, and to the mocking comments of onlookers he replied that if chickens could hatch from boiled eggs, there was nothing strange about sowing boiled beans. Soon King David himself heard of the soldier's strange behavior, and had the man summoned to his palace.

"Who advised you to sow boiled beans?" he asked.

"No one, sire," replied the soldier. "It was my own idea."

"I do not believe it. Solomon must have had a hand in this."

Then the soldier admitted that it was Solomon's idea. David sent for Solomon and said: "I see you are not satisfied with the way I settled the dispute. How, then, would you like to decide the matter?"

"The soldier from your bodyguard cannot be liable for something which does not really exist," said Solomon. "A hen will indeed hatch a chicken from an egg, but never from one that has been cooked in boiling water."

When he heard these words King David summoned the other soldier and changed his judgement: "Whoever has borrowed one boiled egg shall return one boiled egg."

The Death
of David

King David ruled over the whole of Israel for many years. He was wealthy and strong, and the surrounding nations shook before his troops. But neither might nor glory can stave off wrinkles and grey hairs, so even King David grew old, and his thoughts turned more and more to death.

One evening, David was playing his harp. His song rose heavenwards, where it passed through all the gates until it reached God Himself. That day David was singing especially beautifully, and God looked down from Heaven to please His eyes with the sight of His servant. But all of a sudden David put aside his harp and began to pray.

"Lord," he whispered, "how much longer will I play for you? Tell me when I am to die."

"I have decided that creatures of flesh and bone shall not learn the hour of their death," God replied.

"Then tell me," begged David, "the measure of my days."

"That, too, is hidden from all mortals," God told him.

"Then at least tell me the day of the week I shall die on."

And then God said to him: "You shall die on the Jews' day of rest—on the Sabbath."

David tried to persuade God to change His mind. "Oh Lord," he called to Heaven, "let me live one day longer; let me die on Sunday."

"How can I," God replied, "when I have already decreed that on the Sabbath day, when you die, your son Solomon shall take over as ruler of Israel? What I have once decided, no one has the power to change."

"But, Lord, you will surely not mar the holy day with my death?" said David. "Let me die a day earlier, on Friday."

"Can I deprive the world of even one day of your songs of praise?" asked God. "Enough of your bargaining, David: my decision is immutable."

At these words David grew sad. Was he to await the Sabbath with anxiety, the day when all Jews rejoice? With a sad heart he took up his harp again. Suddenly he had an idea. It was known that the Angel of Death had no power over one who was studying the Torah, the book of God's laws. If David were to study the word of God each Sabbath, he would escape death.

From that day on David spent every Sabbath day bent over a scroll of the Torah. From the rising of the first three stars, which signaled the start of the holy day, until the end of the Sabbath, he did not leave his study of God's Word. He penetrated the Holy Book more and more deeply, acquiring an even greater knowledge of the things of God and man; instead of the fear of death he felt with each succeeding Sabbath a joy that he could continue his holy studies. Sabbath after Sabbath David refused to leave the Torah for an instant, so that when the moment came for the King of Israel to give up his soul, the Angel of Death stood helplessly before him. The Sabbath was already drawing to an end, and David still held the holy scroll in his hand. He neither ate nor drank: his eyes remained fixed on the parchment.

Seeing that patience alone was getting him nowhere, the Angel of Death decided to try cunning. The Sabbath when David was to die coincided with the feast of Shabuoth, on which the Jews recalled the day God gave them the Torah and celebrated the ripening of their crops. To the accompaniment of song they would harvest the wheat and barley and fill their baskets with the first figs, grapes, dates, olives and pomegranates. In the garden of David's palace, too, the trees bore their first fruit. The servants were carefully arranging them in gold and silver bowls, and giving thanks to the Creator by singing and dancing and playing pipes and drums. Seeing how David's soul was filled with contentment that God should have favored them so, the Angel of Death crept in among the fruit-gatherers. Unseen, he climbed into the most beautiful of the pomegranate trees, the pride of David's garden, and began to shake the branches with all his might. There was a noise as if a windstorm had struck the garden; it grew dark, and the tree groaned as if in agony, letting its lovely red fruit fall to the ground. Startled, David forgot all about the Torah and ran to the steps leading to the garden to see what disaster had struck his orchard. At that instant the steps gave way beneath him, sending David hurtling towards the ground, where he soon lay dead.

So it was that in the end the Angel of Death triumphed over David. But though his soul had returned to his Maker, David's dead body was not allowed to be buried. It was the Sabbath, the day of rest. David's son Solomon therefore ordered the eagles to hover over his father's body and shade it from the last rays of the sun with their wings. Eagles came from all corners of the earth, and their shadow was the last gift which David received in this world.

The Queen of Sheba's Riddles

When King David died, his son Solomon became King of Israel. He loved God and kept the laws of the Torah, and God looked upon him with favor. One day He appeared to Solomon in a dream and said to him, "Since you are a good steward of my inheritance, I will make you the wisest of men. No mortal shall be your equal, and you shall also have those things which befit the wise: riches and glory."

As God had said, so it came to be. Solomon's wisdom brought him respect, and that respect gave him the strength to govern the whole of a huge empire. He decided all disputes with justice, and the nations learned his proverbs, and sang the songs he composed. God also gave Solomon the power to understand the speech of all animals, and he knew the secrets of all the plants, from the smallest flower which took root on the edge of the desert to the tall cedars; spirits and demons, good and ill, bowed to his commands.

One day King Solomon summoned all the birds of the earth to come to him. Before long the eagles of the rocks and the gulls of the sea, the larks of the field and the vultures of the desert had answered his call. Birds from all corners of the world assembled before his throne.

Then Solomon saw that the wood grouse was missing, and he grew angry: "How dare the wood grouse disobey my command? Bring him here at once, so I can punish him in front of all the other birds!"

But before his servants could set off in search of the wood grouse, he appeared before Solomon of his own accord. "My lord," he said, "forgive me for being late; I was far away, and could not get here sooner."

"Where have you been?" Solomon asked sternly.

"I flew around the world for three months in search of a town which has not yet bowed to your will. Far to the east, in the middle of a great kingdom, there is such a town. It is called Kitor. The stones there are of pure gold, and the roofs of the houses are of silver. There are trees growing there which remember the time God made the world, and their roots are fed by water which springs in the Garden of Eden. The city and the whole empire are ruled over by a woman, who is called the Queen of Sheba. But if you want me to, I will return to Kitor and tell the Queen of Sheba of your might, so that she, too, may bow down before you."

Solomon was pleased with the wood grouse's words. He immediately called his scribes and had a letter written, which he then gave to the wood grouse, telling him to deliver it to the Queen of Sheba as quickly as possible. He also sent the wood grouse an escort — a flock of birds which darkened the sky from horizon to horizon. This strange delegation set off without delay, and before long the Queen of Sheba was holding Solomon's letter in her hand.

"I, Solomon, King of Israel, send you peaceful greetings," he wrote. "God in His grace has made me ruler of all animals, domestic and wild, the birds of the air and the fish of the seas and rivers; demons and spirits likewise obey my will. Kings from all corners of the earth visit me to pay me homage, and I honor them in return. If you come to me, you will be honored too; but if you refuse, I'll send my army to your land. My warriors are rapacious beasts, birds whose wings raise tempests, demons who will strangle you in your beds."

As soon as the Queen of Sheba had read the letter, she summoned her counselors to tell her what to do. "Take no notice of a king we have never heard of," they told her. "Do not go to Solomon, or even reply to him."

But the queen did not take her counselors' advice. Her heart was gripped by anxiety and foreboding. "If he can order the birds to blot out the sky," she thought, "how great the power of the King of Israel must be!" So she ordered her sailors to make ready for a long voyage. She had ships loaded with gold, silver, precious stones, rare woods and much incense; she also chose sixty boys and girls of the same size and age, and had them dressed in crimson robes. When all had been made ready, the Queen of Sheba set out westwards, to Jerusalem, accompanied by her entire court.

As soon as Solomon heard that the Queen of Sheba was approaching, he ordered his servants to take her into a special hall which was made all of crystal. He sat there on a crystal throne, and awaited the entrance of his guest. The queen had never seen glass before, and she thought Solomon was sitting in water, so she raised her robe, revealing her legs.

"Your face is more beautiful than that of any woman I have seen," Solomon greeted the Queen of Sheba. "But your legs are as hairy as a man's."

The Queen of Sheba blushed. "I see you delight in revealing that which is hidden to others," she said, tartly. "You will surely, then, not object to guessing a few riddles. I am curious to see whether your wisdom is as great as people say it is."

Solomon nodded his head. "You may ask them."

"It grows in the fields with its head hung down like reeds. It is the glory of the rich, the shame of the poor, a decoration for the dead and a threat to the living. It brings joy to the birds, but death to fish."

"It is flax," replied Solomon. "Beautiful linen robes are the glory of the rich, linen rags the shame of the poor. The dead are wrapped in a linen shroud, but the flaxen noose on the gallows threatens the living. The birds are happy to find flax, for they eat its seeds, but the fish hate it, for they die in flaxen nets."

"Your answer is correct," said the Queen of Sheba. "Now tell me what water neither

falls from Heaven nor flows from the mountains. Sometimes it is as sweet as honey, sometimes as bitter as wormwood, yet it always comes from the same source."

Solomon replied: "A tear on the cheek neither falls from Heaven nor flows from the mountains. When a man is joyful, his tears are sweet, but tears of sorrow are seven times more bitter."

"The second reply is also correct," said the Queen of Sheba. "But can you guess what gifts I received from my mother? One was born in the sea, the other hidden in the depths of the earth."

"The string of pearls around your neck and the golden ring on your finger will bear witness that I know what you are speaking of," laughed Solomon.

"Then how will you answer the fourth riddle? When it is alive it does not move, but after its death it wanders from place to place."

"Without this thing," Solomon replied, "I should never have seen you. For a ship is made of the wood of a tree which has been felled."

"I have given you four riddles," the Queen of Sheba said, "and you have guessed them all. Allow me to ask another. Who is buried without dying, and after burial comes to life? Those who buried him gain by him."

"Such is the fate of grains of rye and other cereals," Solomon replied.

"And now: who is he who is neither born nor dies?"

"God, ruler of Heaven and Earth, may His name be praised," said Solomon.

The Queen of Sheba bowed to Solomon. "Will you allow me a seventh question, the last?"

"As you wish," Solomon replied.

At these words the Queen of Sheba called in the sixty children she had brought with her from Kitor. "As you can see," she said to Solomon, "the children are of the same age and the same size, and are dressed the same. But some of them are girls and some are boys. Can you say which are which?"

Solomon ordered a sack of nuts to be scattered among the children. The boys unceremoniously lifted their robes and stuffed the nuts into the pockets of the trousers which they wore underneath, while the girls formed their robes into pouches, in which they placed the nuts.

"There are your boys and girls," Solomon pointed, and the Queen of Sheba realized there was not a riddle the King of Israel could not solve. She gave Solomon all the presents she had brought him, and Solomon showered her with gifts in return. None of Solomon's guests had ever been so warmly welcomed, nor did any stay in Jerusalem longer.

"I heard much about you on the way here," the Queen of Sheba told him as they parted, "but now I know that you are even wiser and kinder than people say. Praise be to the god with whom you have found favor, and who has you rule in peace and justice."

The Inquisitive Wife

King Solomon had many admirers, and not a day went by without him receiving one guest at least. Visitors came from near and far, each of them trying to capture the king's imagination. They brought him splendid horses, rare spices and wood; or they simply told of the wisdom of other lands and nations. Of all his guests, Solomon took a particular liking to one man from a country very far away, who traveled to Jerusalem only once a year, bringing with him exotic gifts such as even Solomon had never seen. The King of Israel always rewarded his guest richly, and they both always looked forward to their next meeting.

One year the man gave Solomon a particularly fine present, but would take nothing in return. "Thanks be to God and to your favor, Solomon," he said, "I already have enough for even my grandchildren to live in comfort. But if, my lord, you wish to be generous towards me, then give me something which can neither be seen nor weighed in the hand: teach me to understand the speech of the animals."

Solomon fell sad. "If you were to ask for any other thing," he said, "I should not hesitate to grant it. But what you want to know is like a knife's edge: it may help you, but it may harm you also. If you were to mention the secret to anyone, you would have to die, and no amount of pity could save you."

But Solomon's words only served to make the man more enthusiastic. "If it is only a question of keeping my mouth shut about it, you may rely on me, my lord. Over the years you have known me, you have seen my loyalty for yourself; believe me that you shall not be disappointed in me this time, either. Teach me to understand what the animals are saying!"

Solomon still hesitated; but when he saw how greatly his guest desired this knowledge, and what great delight it would bring him, he did as he was asked. He taught him the secret language of the animals, and on his way home Solomon's visitor was already able to listen to what the birds were saying as they flew from tree to tree.

One day the man was sitting in his courtyard just in front of the stables when his servants brought the ox from the fields. One of the men tied it up at its trough next to an ass, and his master heard through the open door what the two animals said to each other.

"How did you fare today?" asked the ass.

"Well may you ask," replied the ox. "I have been ploughing the fields since dawn, so that I can scarcely put one foot in front of the other, and at daybreak tomorrow my master will drive me out to work again."

"If you were not so stupid," said the ass, "you might take a rest. Look at me — I pretended to be ill, and I have only lain here and slept all day long."

"And how does one pretend to be ill?" the ox asked in surprise.

"All you have to do is not eat the hay the man has prepared for you. When he sees you have left it he will tell the master, and he will think you have a pain somewhere; I am willing to bet that he will give you no work to do tomorrow."

"What fine advice the ass is giving round here!" the animals' master thought to himself, amused. He waited a while, and when he heard no sound coming from the stables, he went in. When he looked towards the trough, what should he see — the ox had taken the

ass's advice and left his hay untouched. He had just fallen asleep with exhaustion. But the ass was not idle, and the moment his companion's eyes were closed, he set to and ate the ox's share.

The master laughed out loud. "That ass of mine is a fine one, but he shall not get the better of me." And he called one of the servants and told him to let the ox rest the next day, and to harness the ass to the plough in his place. Then the master returned to the house in a merry mood. But the moment he stepped into the parlor, his wife started getting at him.

"I heard you laughing out there. What did you find so funny, unless it was more of your scheming? You only laugh at me all the time, and you suppose I don't know it."

"Whatever are you thinking of, wife," the man defended himself. "I only recalled a tale that King Solomon told me."

"Then tell me about it, too," his wife demanded.

Taken unawares, the man could think of nothing, and his wife began to shout: "I thought as much! You didn't remember a thing — you were laughing at me, and you are only using Solomon as an excuse!" She shouted at him more and more, grew angry and reviled him, until there was nothing he could do but make off in shame like a proven liar.

The next evening the man again went to sit by the stables, so that he might hear what the animals said to each other. A servant led the ass from the fields, and the creature, exhausted from the unaccustomed toil, collapsed in a heap beside the ox.

"You advised me well," the ox told him gratefully. "I have not had such a fine time for ages. I had a good sleep, and the servants looked after me all day. I only hope my illness lasts a long time!"

"Do not be so hasty," gasped the worn-out ass. "I heard the master speaking in the fields. He said it was a pity for an animal like me to pull the plough. If you do not begin to eat and plough the way you used to, he will soon have you slaughtered for meat!"

As soon as the ox heard this, he leapt to his feet and began to feed as fast as he could. The man, who had heard and seen everything, began to laugh at the ass's cunning. He laughed until he was quite out of breath; then, suddenly, his wife was standing there in front of him.

"Was it not enough for you to laugh at me yesterday?" she snapped. "Am I to be a laughing-stock every day? I vow you shall be less dear to me than the beggar at our gate, unless you tell me what you were laughing at."

"My dear wife," he replied, quietly, "you know you are dear to me, and that I should never harm you. Believe me, I was not laughing at you; but I can tell you no more than that, for if I were to reveal one word of the truth, I should die. As you love me, take back your vow, and do not torment me with further questions."

"Why should I take back my vow?" his wife cried, angrily. "What reason have I to believe you? I want to know what you were laughing at, and I should rather die myself than have my question left unanswered!"

The man was horrified. "You would set your life against my silence? Then I shall be the one to die. I will answer your question, but now you must leave me alone. I shall make my will and take my leave of my friends."

At that the husband and wife parted, and the man pondered gloomily how Solomon's warning was proving to be justified. "I thought there was nothing simpler than to be silent," he said bitterly. "But now I am not only going to break my promise to the King of Israel, but to die into the bargain."

As he sat meditating thus, all the animals on his farm got to hear of his conversation with his wife. The one who grieved most for his master was his dog. Out of misery at the thought that his master must die, he could neither eat nor drink the water in his bowl. When the cock saw that the dog had left his meat and water, he called all the hens and they ate the food together.

The dog turned on the cock: "How can you be so insensitive?" he barked angrily. "At any moment your master must die for his sin, and you have no thought other than your own comfort!"

The cock looked at the dog in surprise: "And what do you expect me to do? If the master is foolish, then he must expect to pay for it. Look at me — I have ten wives, and I get along with all of them; none of them would dare defy my will. The master has learnt little from the wise Solomon, if he cannot even handle his own wife. If he were to give her a sound beating she would certainly not love him the less for it, and she would care a good deal less to know the secrets of men."

The cock shouted this out to the whole courtyard, and his voice reached the master's ears. The man was at the end of his strength, but when he heard the cock's advice, it was as if he had suddenly grown younger. He leapt up, did as the cock had suggested, and has lived with his wife ever since in harmony and without strife. On his next visit to Jerusalem he told Solomon the whole story.

"Be grateful to the cock for helping you cure your wife's curiosity!" laughed the King of Israel. "For it is better to live in a corner on the roof than under the same roof with a shrewish wife."

The Three
Loaves

During the reign of the wise King Solomon, a certain poor woman lived in a tiny cottage by the sea. Her husband had long since died, and her children had gone their different ways, so she had no one to bring her joy in her old age. From morning till evening she mended the fishermen's nets. It did not bring in much money — just enough for her not to go hungry and to save a little flour for the winter, when the fishermen did not go out because of the wind and rain that lashed the sea. But she never complained of her lot. People liked her, and a kind word here and there was comfort enough to her in her solitude.

But one year the winter was longer than usual. Great waves came up on the sea, and the fishermen were not able to go out. None of them needed his nets repaired, and as the days went by the woman's store of flour in the larder grew smaller and smaller. When there was not enough of it left to bake even a griddle cake, she set out to visit the richest man in the village.

"What do you want?" he asked her.

"I am starving," the woman replied. "Give me a little flour, I beseech you, so that I may get through this cruel winter."

"I should like to help you," replied the rich man, "but I have just sold the last sack. I have only enough left for myself and my family. But if you can manage with what is left on the floor of my store-room, you are welcome to it."

The woman thanked him, carefully swept the whole store-room, and went home happily with a little bag of flour. Right away she lit a fire under the oven and started to make some dough. Before long she was drawing out of the oven three beautiful, golden-brown loaves of bread. Night was falling, and because the woman had not eaten since morning, she was very hungry indeed. Quickly, she picked up one of the loaves, and was just about to bless it and cut herself a good slice from it, when a stranger knocked at the door. He was dressed in rags, and was so exhausted he could hardly speak. "Good woman," he begged her, "give me something to eat. I am a merchant, but I was attacked on the road by robbers; they took everything I had and I was lucky to escape with my life. It is a whole age since I last ate, and I am at the end of my strength."

The stranger had scarcely finished speaking before the woman handed him the first of her loaves. "Take this bread," she said, "and God be with you."

The man thanked her, and went his way. "He needed the bread more than I," thought the woman to herself. "And anyway I still have two loaves," and she picked up the second loaf; but just at that moment there was another knock on the door. The woman opened it, and there on the threshold was a traveler even more tattered than the one to whom she had given the first loaf.

"Good woman," the stranger said weakly, "my whole house has burnt down, and I have become a beggar overnight. Though I escaped the flames, I am now dying of hunger. You can see that I can scarcely walk: I beg of you, do not turn me away without food."

The woman did not hesitate: she gave the stranger the second loaf, wished him good fortune, and returned to the table to eat herself. "This poor man was also hungrier than I," she said to herself. "It is lucky that I baked three loaves." And she picked up the third loaf impatiently; but before she had spoken the words of the blessing over it, a strong wind got up outside. It swirled round the house, flung the door open and, before the old woman knew what was happening, snatched the loaf from her hands. A whirlwind lifted it up into the air and carried it out to sea.

Now the woman burst into tears. "Wind, how can you be so cruel?" she cried. "I gave two loaves to beggars, and when at last I want to eat myself, you have to come along and take my last mouthful! What use is my bread to the sea?"

All night the woman did not sleep a wink. She thought whom she might have wronged; but her conscience was so clear that, try as she might, she could think of no reason why she should be punished so. When the sun rose, she resolved to take her cause to King Solomon, and make a complaint against the wind. "Solomon is the wisest man in the world," she said to herself. "No one else can judge my dispute with the wind."

Solomon listened carefully to what the woman had to say. He asked her about everything which had happened to her in her life, and in the end he said: "If you want to lay this charge against the wind, you must wait until I summon him this evening. He must be present, and I cannot disturb him just now, for he is blowing into the merchants' sails. But wait here until he comes, and then I will decide your case."

The woman stood to one side, and three merchants came and knelt before the royal throne. "King of Israel," they said, "allow us to ask a charitable act of you. Accept these seven thousand gold pieces from us, and give them to some poor man, one whose nobility makes him worthy of them."

"Why are you making this gift?" Solomon asked.

"For love of God and gratitude for His providence," answered the oldest of the merchants. "If you will bear with me a while, my lord, I will explain to you." The merchant pointed to the chest containing the seven thousand gold pieces, and said: "This sum is exactly a tenth part of the value of the cargo our ship was carrying. As we neared the shores of your kingdom, a tempest arose. The waves tossed our ship about like a small piece of timber; we lost our bearings, and to make matters worse a crack opened up in the side of the vessel. It was not a large one, but the ship was taking in more and more water, and in the midst of the raging elements we were not able to find anything to stop up the hole.

In our despair we prayed to God, and vowed that if we should be delivered from our peril we would give to the poor a tenth part of the value of our cargo. Soon the storm died down, the waves calmed, and we reached the shore in safety. We calculated one tenth of the value of our cargo, and it was exactly seven thousand gold pieces. This is the sum we have brought to you, asking that you give it to the poor according to your judgement."

"I shall be glad to do as you ask," Solomon replied. "But one thing remains unexplained. You said that a crack opened up in the side of your ship. A vessel which is holed will sink even in the calmest of seas, yet you remained afloat. How do you explain that?"

At these words the merchant thrust his hand into a fold in his cloak and took out a battered, waterlogged loaf of bread. "This," said the merchant, "was suddenly brought by the wind. The force of the gale blew it into the hole in the hull of our ship, and only thus were we saved."

"It seems that the loaf which was of such assistance to you has just come back to its true owner," laughed Solomon, and he turned to the old woman. "Do you recognize your property?"

"Indeed: that is the very loaf which the wind snatched from me," replied the woman, surprised.

"In that case," said Solomon, "the seven thousand gold pieces are also yours. God did not forget your charity, and he ordered the wind not to leave you in distress. You wished to sue the wind for a wrong against you; but what seemed to be misfortune has now turned out to be good fortune. You will never know want again."

The news of this strange incident soon spread throughout the kingdom, and all praised the divine justice and wisdom of Solomon, King of Israel.

✡

The Site
of the Temple

King Solomon inherited great riches from his father, David, and through wise government increased them still further. None of his plans remained unaccomplished, and his glory filled the earth. Nonetheless, Solomon remained sad.

"What use are all these riches to me," he said to himself bitterly, "when the years pass by, and I have still not fulfilled the promise I gave my Father? I have had dozens of palaces built, yet there is still no temple in honor of God. But God is my witness that it is not through ill will that I have delayed the building. How am I to know which place is most fitting for the temple to be built? The whole of the land of Israel is holy, but the ground upon which the walls of God's temple are to rise must be the dearest of all to Him."

One night Solomon was lying awake worrying about where the temple should be built. When midnight passed and he had still not fallen asleep, Solomon decided to get up and take a walk. He dressed quickly. Quietly, so that none of the servants might see him, he stole out of the palace and strode through the quiet streets of Jerusalem, passing great gardens and groves whose leaves rustled in the wind, until his steps took him to Mount Moria. It was just after harvesting time, and sheaves of freshly-mown wheat were standing on the southern slopes of the hill. Solomon leaned against the trunk of an olive tree and closed his eyes. The images of different parts of his kingdom went through his mind. He saw the hills, valleys and groves which he had once believed would become the site of the temple, and he saw also the dozens of other corners of his land where he had arrived full of hope and left disappointed.

Suddenly Solomon heard footsteps. Opening his eyes, he saw in the moonlight a man carrying a sheaf of wheat. "A thief!" thought the king. He was about to step out of his hiding place in the shade of the tree, but then decided to stay where he was. "I had better wait," he said to himself, "and see what this fellow is up to."

The man worked quickly and quietly. He carried the sheaf to the edge of the neighboring field, then returned for another, and continued in this way until he had transferred fifty sheaves. He then looked around timidly, and as soon as he was sure no one had spotted him, went away again.

"A fine neighbor," thought Solomon. "The owner of the field must wonder why his harvest gets smaller in the night."

But before Solomon had even decided how the thief should be punished, a second man appeared close to the tree under which he stood. He cautiously walked round both fields, and as soon as he was sure he was alone, he grabbed a sheaf of wheat and took it from one field to the other. He did exactly as the first had done, except that he carried the sheaves in the opposite direction. When he had moved fifty of them, he, too, slipped away.

"Each of the neighbors is better than the other," Solomon said to himself. "I thought only one of them was stealing, but I see that robber robs robber."

The next morning the king sent for the owners of the two fields. He told the elder to wait in an adjacent chamber, and turned sternly towards the younger: "Tell me what right you have to take grain from your neighbor's field."

The man looked at Solomon in amazement, and reddened with shame. "Sire," he replied, "I should never do such a thing. The grain I move is my own, and I take it to my brother's field. I wanted no one to know of it, but since I am discovered, I will tell you, King Solomon, the truth. My brother and I inherited from our father the same portions of field, though he has a wife and three children and I live alone. My brother needs the grain more than I, but he will not take a single stalk from me. So I take the sheaves to him in secret. I can do without them, and he can use them."

Solomon sent the first man into the adjacent chamber and called in the second. "Why do you steal from your neighbor?" he asked in a harsh voice. "I know you take away his grain at night."

"God forbid that I should ever do such a thing," gasped the man, startled. "The opposite is the case, Solomon. My brother and I inherited equal portions of field from our father, but I have a wife and three children to help me with my work, while he is alone. He has to employ reapers, binders and flailers, so that he spends more money than I, and therefore needs more grain. But he refuses to take any from me, so I give him a few sheaves in secret. I shall not miss them, and they may be of use to him."

When he heard this, Solomon called the first brother back into his chamber, embraced both of them, and said, "I have seen many things in my life, but I have never met brothers as unselfish as you. For years you have been acting charitably and hiding the fact from each other. I admire you, and I beg your pardon that I suspected you, the noblest men in the land, of theft. But now I have a request to make of you: sell me your fields, for it is on them, consecrated as they are with brotherly love, that I would build the temple of God. There is no other place more worthy, and the temple could have no sounder foundations."

The brothers were delighted. They gave him their fields, and the King of Israel rewarded them generously. He gave them in addition fields which were larger and more fertile, and he had it proclaimed throughout the land that a site had been found for the temple of God.

Solomon
and Ashmodai

Before Solomon began building the temple in honor of the one God, he made careful preparations. He had large stocks of granite and marble assembled for the walls, and the King of Tyre sent cedar and cypress for the inside cladding. Famous architects drew up plans for the temple, and thousands of laborers from all sides of the kingdom made their way to the site. But King Solomon was still not satisfied, and the more he thought about the temple, the more anxious he became. According to the law of Israel no iron was to be used in a sacred building, for the metal was an instrument of destruction and death. But how were they to hew the great blocks of stone without iron?

Solomon pondered this question day and night, but for once his wisdom failed him, and his pious heart was unable to help. When he could find no way around the problem, he called together his wise men and asked their advice.

"Wisest of kings," the oldest of the wise men began, "ten things came into being at twilight on the sixth day of creation. One of these was the shamir, a tiny worm whose mere touch is enough to split the hardest marble or granite. If you can obtain a shamir, then you can build a temple to the glory of God and Israel, even without iron implements."

"Your words have raised my spirits," answered Solomon. "But do you also know where the wondrous shamir lives, and how to get it?"

"No mortal can answer that question," the wise man replied. "It is said that the shamir has stayed in the Garden of Eden since the Creation; but I have also heard that it is to be found in the distant and desolate places ruled over by demons. You must ask them. Maybe they will help you."

As soon as the wise men had left, Solomon shut himself up in his royal chamber and called up two demons. "You have come at my command," he addressed them. "Grant me, then, another wish. I want to build a temple to my God, and I need the shamir worm to break up the stone. You have knowledge beyond that of man. Tell me where the shamir lives, and how I am to get it."

"We know of the powers of the wondrous shamir," replied the demons, "but the secret of its life is hidden from us. It is guarded by our ruler, the mighty Ashmodai."

"Where can I find him?" asked Solomon.

The demons were silent, but Solomon persisted, and they finally spoke again: "Far away from here, far from Jerusalem, stands a high mountain. Beneath it Ashmodai dug a well, which he filled with pure spring water. So that the water might not become tainted or warmed by the rays of the sun, he covered the well with a stone top, upon which each day he sets his seal. Then Ashmodai flies up from the earth and stops before the throne of God. There he listens to the celestial music and the angels' song of praise, and delights in the view of far-off worlds and stars. Towards evening Ashmodai flies right across the heavens, and when the sun sets beyond the sea he returns to his well. He examines the seal carefully, and if it is unbroken, he refreshes himself with the cooling water. Then he rests until daybreak, when he once again sets out on his daily journey."

The demons vanished, and Solomon returned to his court. He held all his subjects in esteem, but his favorite was a captain of the guard called Benayash, a young man as handsome as he was valiant. Solomon called him and told him of all he had learnt from the wise men and the demons. Finally he said to him: "Benayash, I have no finer soldier than you; whom else, then, should I send to capture Ashmodai and bring him to Jerusalem? Have you the courage to set yourself against the king of the demons?"

"I will do all that you ask," the young man replied, pleased to have earned his monarch's praise and favor. He bowed down low, and that very day set out at the head of a small force of horsemen on the long journey. On Solomon's advice he took with him spades, shovels, a bag of the finest sheep's wool, and the sweetest and most aromatic wine from the best of the king's vineyards, together with a decorated casket containing a golden chain, on each link of which was written God's name. Thus equipped, after a long and difficult trek, Benayash reached Ashmodai's mountain. The sun was only just beginning its climb across the heavens, so Benayash had time enough to put his plan into action.

First of all he had a deep pit dug in the ground below the level of Ashmodai's well. Into this he drained the water from the well through an underground channel, and had the hole in the well stopped up with wool. Then Benayash's companions dug a second pit with an underground channel, this time higher up than the well. Into this one they poured the wine they had brought, and it ran down into Ashmodai's well. Then Solomon's soldiers carefully removed all traces of their work, concealed themselves in the foliage of the trees, and awaited Ashmodai's return.

As the last of the sun's rays faded, a sudden darkness fell, and the trees were shaken by a mighty gust of wind. At once the heavens were sundered by a fiery lightning flash, and close to the well there appeared, borne on brilliant blue wings, a huge creature, far taller than the tallest of the trees. Ashmodai had returned to earth from his long day's travels. Benayash and his companions had to use all their strength to cling to the branches. They were terrified.

The king of demons went up to the well and examined his seal carefully. When he found it was still intact, he pushed aside the heavy stone cover with a single movement of his huge arm. He bent over the surface of the water, then leapt back in surprise.

"How did wine get into my well?" he called out in amazement. "Does it not dull the senses? Does it not harm the wise more than the venom of snakes?"

Ashmodai turned away from the well in anger, but his thirst got the better of him.

"I shall only wet my palate," he said to himself. "At least I shall find out what it is that brings men such pleasure." He filled his cupped hands with wine and took a sip. Then he thrust his hands back into the well to drink again, and again and again, more and more quickly and impatiently.

Solomon had known what he was doing when he chose the wine for Ashmodai. There was no drink on earth more delicious, but none more stupefying, either. So when Ashmodai had drunk the wine from the well to the last drop, he fell helplessly to the ground and dropped into a deep sleep. This was the moment Benayash had been waiting for. He climbed down from the tree, took from the casket the chain whose links bore the name of God, and cautiously hung it around the demon's neck. The moment the precious metal touched Ashmodai's skin, a wondrous transformation took place. The demon king's body gave a jerk, and then began to grow smaller. Ashmodai was soon no bigger than an ordinary mortal. Benayash then bound him hand and foot with strong cords, and kept watch beside his prisoner till daybreak.

No sooner had the clouds in the eastern sky taken on the rosy tint of early morning, than Ashmodai awoke. With a sudden heave he burst the bonds on his hands and feet, as if he had been tied up with blades of grass instead of stout rope; then he let out a cry of pain. His shout set the trees quivering, flinging Benayash and his fellows to the ground. But the demon could not rid himself of the chain bearing the seal of God. In vain did he strain his muscles: his efforts to free himself were futile. The slender chain lay heavy on his shoulders. As soon as Ashmodai realized that no amount of effort or lamentation would help him, he yielded to Benayash's will and set off with him to Jerusalem.

A glorious welcome awaited Benayash in the royal city. King Solomon set him in the place of honor at the banquet table, and had him recount the whole affair in great detail. Finally, the captive Ashmodai was brought in. When he saw Solomon, he drew on the ground with a stick a rectangle the size of a man, and said in a bitter voice, "When you die, you will have no more than a piece of ground like that. Are you not satisfied with the power you have already? Will you have my sceptre, too?"

"Mighty king of the demons," Solomon replied. "I did not have you brought to Jerusalem to pander to my own ambition. I was led to do so by reverence for God, who is your God, too. I wish to build a temple worthy of His greatness, and to do so I need the shamir worm in order to work the stones. Tell me where I can find it, and how to get it. That is all I ask of you."

The king's words assuaged the demon's anger. "Very well, Solomon, I will tell you what I know of the shamir. After the Creation God gave it to the prince of the waters and seas. But the prince did not keep the shamir. He placed it in the care of a large bird, and the new keeper of the wonderful worm was made to swear that she would never allow anyone to take it. The bird's nest can be found in a bare cliff face in the middle of a great desert, hidden from view in a cave. That is where you must seek the worm."

Ashmodai's words were as sweet music to Solomon's ears. He sent for Benayash at once, and asked him to set out on a new journey. After receiving the king's blessing, Benayash quickly made ready to depart, and left Jerusalem with a small company to go in search of the bird and the shamir.

Benayash and his men traveled for weeks and months, leaving behind them ever more desolate and solitary countryside. When they finally reached the edge of the desert, they looked around impatiently for the goal of their journey. But the hoofprints of King Solomon's horses stretched wide across the sands before Benayash found the cliff Ashmodai had told him about. Almost at the top, the soldiers found the hidden cave where the bird had her nest. The bird-guardian of the shamir was not there; only her young stretched their hungry throats out of the nest, waiting for their mother to return with some food. "Where there are children," said Benayash to himself, "the mother must soon return. It is no great task to catch the bird, but how am I to find the shamir?" He thought for a while, then ordered the soldiers to roll a big stone in front of the entrance to the cave. Then he and his friends hid behind the rocks.

It was not long before the bird arrived. As if out of nowhere, she came flying up with a beakful of food. She alighted in front of the cave, then noticed the boulder separating her from her young. Dropping the food from her beak, she attacked the boulder ferociously. But, try as she might, the hard stone was too much for her beak. The bird tried once more: with a croaking cry she flung herself against the boulder and tried to roll it away with her wings. All to no avail. In the end she did what Benayash had expected her to do. She rose into the air and made for a narrow crevice, through which no man could have passed. The bird disappeared inside and emerged carrying the shamir in her beak. It was enough to place the worm against the stone and the boulder split into a thousand fragments. That was the moment Benayash chose to leap out of his hiding place with a loud cry. The bird gave a start and dropped the shamir, and before she could recover, Benayash was holding the wonderful worm between his fingers.

When Benayash returned to Jerusalem, the whole city rejoiced. Now there was nothing to prevent work on the temple from going ahead. In the fourth year of his reign, Solomon, with the help of the shamir, had the first stones worked for the foundations; in the eleventh year of his reign all the work was finished. Throughout the seven years neither the ring of a hammer nor the sound of chisels or other iron tools was heard on the building site. All was done according to the prescriptions of the Torah and in a manner pleasing to God. For the consecration of the temple Solomon summoned a meeting of the elders of Israel and representatives from all the twelve tribes. Together they brought out the ark containing the tablets on which was inscribed the covenant between God and the people of Israel. They placed the covenant in the sanctuary beneath the wings of cherubs made of olive wood. And all the Jews admired the splendor of the temple, for none of them had ever seen a building so magnificent. On its walls were flowers and chalices carved from cedar wood, and it was hung with silken curtains, with fastenings of precious stones. All the objects in the temple were made of gold, silver, copper or bronze, skilfully decorated with engraved palms, pomegranates and lions. Solomon knelt, raised his hands to heaven, and prayed to God not to desert His people, to hear the pleas of those who turned to the holy temple.

But it came to pass that King Solomon himself forgot his humility. The riches which God had heaped upon the King of Israel's head as the crown of wisdom seemed rather to draw a veil across his eyes. Solomon built a fleet which constantly brought him new gold, silver, ivory, precious stones, balsams, spices and rare woods, heaped up robes and armor, bought horses, monkeys, peacocks. Caravans loaded with goods were arriving in Jerusalem daily, and the king was drowning in luxury. He surrounded himself with dancers, musicians and noble guests; he was proud that he could answer all their questions.

"I am not only the richest and most powerful, but also the cleverest of men," Solomon would congratulate himself when his visitors had left. But then one day he remembered Ashmodai, whom he still held captive, and his joy melted away. What were all the riddles of men compared to the secrets of the king of the demons!

One day, as Benayash was taking Solomon and Ashmodai to Jerusalem, they passed by a wedding, and the demon king began to weep. They passed a man who was ordering enough shoes from a cobbler to last for seven years, and Ashmodai laughed. They saw a magician trying to conjure up a treasure, and Ashmodai laughed again. What did all this mean? How was Solomon to explain such strange behavior?

The king thought about this for days and nights on end, but he still could not find the answer. Reluctantly, he had the demon brought to him, and when they were alone and no one could hear what was said, he asked Ashmodai to explain.

"When I saw the wedding procession," Ashmodai told him, "I wept because I knew that the young husband would be dead by sunset. I laughed at the man who wanted shoes for seven years, for no one can be sure of the next seven days of his life. And how

could I help laughing at the magician, when the treasure he intended to conjure up was hidden beneath the stone he was sitting on?"

"If Ashmodai has such wisdom when he is in bonds," thought Solomon, "how mighty he must be without them!" Ashmodai read his thought. "O mighty king," he said, "with my help you have become the most admired of mortals. But with this chain around my neck I am able to do only a fraction of the things I am otherwise capable of. Take off the chain, and lend me for a moment your holy ring. I will reveal all secrets to you; I will make your glory reach to the heavens themselves!"

Blinded by ambition, Solomon agreed without hesitation. He approached Ashmodai, took the chain which bore the name of God and slipped off his own ring, the ring with the divine seal upon it, once given to him in his sleep by the Archangel Michael. But he had no sooner placed the ring in Ashmodai's hand, than the king of the demons grew into a giant. He straightened up to the whole of his enormous height, seized the King of Israel and hurled him a thousand miles away. Then he flung the ring into the deepest ocean, took on the form of Solomon, and began to rule over the kingdom of Israel.

Solomon landed in a strange country, not far from a royal palace. He had himself announced at once, and when the local ruler received him, he explained who he was, and asked him for a horse and an escort for his journey back to Jerusalem.

"That renowned city is somewhere to the east," said the unknown monarch. "I have heard of it, and of the wisdom of its ruler. But if you are truly the King of Israel, I know no reason why I should help you. Or are you more reliant on strangers than on yourself and your God?"

The monarch gave a wave of his hand, and the guards led Solomon from the palace.

"Very well," said Solomon to himself, resentfully. "If the king will not help me, then someone else will." But neither merchants nor the soldiers who traveled from land to land were willing to help him. In vain did Solomon command them; in vain did he try to persuade them. All he got in reply was ridicule and disdain. Fortunately, he had a small piece of gold about his person, and he was able to buy food with the money he obtained in return for it. But within a day his purse was empty, and in order not to starve Solomon had to sell his sumptuous royal robes for a pittance. What a transformation! He, who was used to garments embroidered with gold and silver, was obliged to wear next to his skin a pair of patched trousers and a tattered shirt. He, who had once sat astride the noblest horses, now, barefoot, had to drive a scraggy mule. His hand, which had been kissed in homage by thousands, now gripped a soiled linen bag containing scraps of dry bread. His body, unused to the rigors of a long journey, began to waste away, and every step was torture to the king.

Three years it took Solomon to plod his way home; for more than a thousand days he had not seen the golden city. At last he saw before him the temple to God. A soldier was standing guard at the foot of one of its pillars. "In foreign parts they did not know me," thought Solomon, "but here I am at home. My people will receive me."

Solomon laid a hand on the guard's shoulder. "Rejoice," he told him. "Solomon, your king, is returned."

The soldier stared at Solomon uncomprehendingly. "Our monarch has never been away," he said. "But if you wish, you may go to the palace. I'll get you the escort you deserve."

He pushed Solomon along in front of him, and called out: "Behold the king! The king of the beggars craves audience!"

It did not take long for a jeering crowd to gather; they shouted at Solomon, and threw mud at him. They made such a row that the captain of the guard himself came out to see what was going on. When Solomon saw him, he was startled. He had expected to see his faithful Benayash, but instead a total stranger stood there at the palace gate.

"By what right have you taken the place of Benayash?" cried Solomon. "I am the only one with the right to decide matters of rank!"

The crowd began to laugh, but the captain of the guard stilled them with a snap of his fingers. "Are there two Gods in heaven," he asked threateningly, "who have made a covenant with Israel? Two Holy Lands? Two Jerusalems and two temples, for the chosen people to be governed by two kings?"

"As there is one God," cried Solomon, proudly, "one Holy Land, one Jerusalem and one temple, so I am the one King of Israel — I, Solomon, son of David!"

"How dare you say such a thing? Can the cuckoo, which lays her eggs in others' nests, claim that under the wings of an eagle her eggs will hatch into the king of birds? The shell will crack and the truth will out. And you, in a beggar's rags, would claim in the holy city to be king? Get rid of him!"

Dozens of hands tried to seize Solomon, and the son of David was glad to escape with his life. It was only now that his true torment began; for what is bodily weariness compared to the pain of the soul? What are sore feet compared to emptiness of the mind? How bitterly Solomon regretted his own reckless greed, and how great was his desire to enter the temple! He fell prostrate, as he had when the temple was consecrated. This time he was not in front of the congregation, but all alone, in the depths of his own heart.

Then Solomon left Jerusalem and came to another city. His steps took him to the market-place, and there, lost in sad thought, he watched the purchasers idly. One of them turned to Solomon, asking him to help carry the figs he had bought; Solomon agreed.

The man Solomon went with was the cook in a rich household. Solomon was given a meal for his pains, and the cook asked him if he would like to work as his assistant. Solomon was glad to accept the offer. Early the next morning he began work. He made ready the firewood for the stove, peeled the potatoes, cleaned the fruit, washed the pots and pans, and did the shopping in the market.

After he had worked in the house for a year, Solomon went again one day to buy figs in the market. On the way there he met the richest man in the city. He looked at Solomon and said, "Were you not once King of Israel? Oh, how are the mighty fallen!" Solomon walked on in silence; he bought the figs and set off home. In front of the door of the house a beggar was sitting. As Solomon passed him, the beggar bowed and said, "Are you not Solomon, builder of the temple? What God has taken, He will return." Again Solomon did not speak. He gave the cook the figs and began cleaning fish. One of them was particularly large. Solomon cut it open, and saw that there was another, quite small fish inside. He was about to throw it out, when he noticed a small round lump beneath its skin. Filled with curiosity, he cut open the second fish, and — what a surprise! Inside gleamed his golden ring bearing the seal of God, which Ashmodai had thrown into the sea.

Solomon went at once to the cook, thanked him, and said farewell; then he put the ring on his hand. As soon as the band of gold was on his finger, its wonderful powers took him to Jerusalem, right into the midst of a gathering of the wisest men of Israel. And who should be standing before them but Benayash, who had strange things to relate. He told them how, more than four years before, the king had suddenly changed his ways, had turned against his favorites. Benayash himself had fallen out of favor, and was forced to flee, and to go into hiding for a long while. Stranger still, the king had started to be most careful to prevent anyone from seeing his legs. But before Benayash had left, he had managed to take a furtive peep by turning back a corner of the royal raiment. The legs he had seen were not a man's legs at all, but those of a cock — like the legs of a demon that has taken on human form.

The assembly was overcome with horror, which increased when Solomon stepped out in front of them. The ring had brought back to him his majestic aspect and his kingly resolve. All who were present recognized their sovereign, and the whole assembly fell to its knees.

Then, at the head of a huge procession, Solomon entered the royal palace. The servants knelt before him, and the guards stepped aside to let him pass. Thus Solomon came to the hall where Ashmodai sat enthroned. When he saw Solomon with the holy ring upon his finger, his face twisted with rage. Then, in front of everyone's eyes, Ashmodai grew wings, and in an instant a huge demon had flown out of the palace with a loud shriek.

Solomon ruled Israel for forty years in all, but he feared Ashmodai until his dying day. At night the king's ring ceased to act as protection against demons. And so it is written in the *Song of Solomon:*

> "Look; it is Solomon carried on his litter;
> sixty of Israel's chosen warriors
> are his escort,
> all of them skilled swordsmen,
> all trained to handle arms,
> each with his sword ready at his side
> to ward off the demon of the night."

The Fox
as Advocate

It so happened that the lion grew angry with all the animals for their disobedience, and they in their fear were looking for someone to plead their case. No one wanted the task except the fox, who offered his services gladly. "Come along with me," he told the other animals. "I know three hundred fables, and they will appease our king."

The animals were delighted, and they all set off to see the lion. After they had gone some distance, the fox suddenly stopped. "What has happened?" the animals asked anxiously.

"I have just forgotten a hundred fables," replied the fox.

"No matter," said the other animals. "Two hundred will be plenty for the lion."

So they all set off again, but before long the fox stopped again. "Imagine," he said, looking ashamed, "I have forgotten another hundred fables."

"It can't be helped," the animals replied. "Anyway, you still have a hundred. Let's hurry, so the lion won't be even angrier with us."

Soon the animals were standing before the lion's den. A terrible growling came from inside, and the animals began to shake with fear. "An unfortunate thing has happened," whispered the fox. "I cannot remember a single fable. You will have to get along without me. Let everyone answer for his own faults, and speak as best he can!"

The Stupid Ass

One day the lion, king of the animals, decided to sail away with his entire court to far-off lands. He summoned the ass and said to him, "I entrust you with the task of collecting taxes from all the passengers. Go, now, and obey my command."

So the ass stood by the gangplank and asked all the animals for money. When the fox came, he wanted to board the ship free. "How dare you ask me for money?" he shouted at the ass. "Don't you know that the king's escort need not pay?"

"The lion said nothing about that," replied the ass. "Indeed, he ordered me to collect taxes from all the passengers, so I shouldn't even allow *him* to board the ship free. Isn't all the money his anyway?"

The fox went away angrily and asked for an audience with the lion at once. When he told the lion what the ass had said, the lion flew into a rage. He ordered the ass to be slain for his disrespect, and told the fox to prepare the creature's meat for a feast. The fox did as he was told, and began to cook. But he was very hungry, and could not resist eating the ass's heart. At the feast the lion noticed this immediately.

"How could you have the effrontery to deprive me of the ass's heart?" he asked the fox, angrily.

"Forgive me, mighty king," the fox replied, meekly, "but any animal foolish enough to want to collect tax from the king cannot have had a heart."

The lion laughed at the fox's clever reply, and did not punish him.

THE THIRD
LIGHT

The Prophet
Elijah

The Retribution
of Elijah

In olden times there lived in the Holy Land a man named Elijah the Tishbite. God regarded him with great favor, and conferred upon him a power which other men do not have: Elijah could see into the future. He was therefore called Elijah the Prophet.

From morning till night Elijah would go from place to place teaching his fellow Jews the way of wisdom, love and truth. His sparkling, all-seeing eyes struck fear into many a scoundrel. But good folk loved Elijah, and he never let them down. When a poor man had nothing to eat, Elijah would secretly fill his sacks with flour. When a child was troubled with fever, Elijah would appear by its bedside and place his hand on its burning forehead, and the fearful sickness would disappear. No one saw Elijah do these things, but everyone knew he had been there.

Elijah lived very modestly. His home was in a cave on Mount Carmel, and he had only a single animal hide tied with a belt for clothing. His only other possession was a gnarled old staff. When he traveled he ate only fruit he picked from trees, or the food he received from those good folk who offered him shelter for the night.

Joel, who owned large fields on Mount Carmel, was quite the opposite — a rich man out and out. He grew splendid melons on his land, and these had brought him such a reputation that he had plenty of property and money. In spite of this, he never spared a thought for the poor, and would drive travelers away from his gates.

When Elijah heard of the way Joel behaved, he decided to convince him of the truth. Taking on the guise of an old beggar, he set out for Joel's house. There was great merrymaking in the rich man's household that day, for Joel's only daughter was getting married. Joel did everything he could to ensure that the wedding would be one that was talked of for a long time. He invited the richest people for miles around, and employed cooks from foreign places to prepare dozens of exotic dishes. Every room was decorated with masses of flowers, a different color for each room. One room was filled with red blossoms, another shone with yellow, a third was all blue, others all shades of pink and violet, and the whole house was filled with fragrance. Joel had a broad carpet laid from his house to that of the bridegroom, so that no one in the wedding party need touch the ground at all; for the groom himself he had a silver-ornamented litter made. The bride's dress was woven from golden thread, and her ring took the best goldsmith in Jerusalem a whole month to make.

As soon as the marriage ceremony was over, the great banquet began. The guests praised the skills of the foreign cooks, wine flowed like water, and all who came to Joel's house admired the wealth of their host, and rejoiced and made merry. When the entertainment was in full swing, Elijah appeared among the guests. No one saw him enter Joel's house; he was just suddenly there. The prophet was dressed in sackcloth; a threadbare bag lay across his shoulders, and his untidy hair fell over his brow.

Joel did not recognize his visitor. "What do you want here?" he asked roughly, turning to Elijah. "There is nothing to spare, especially not for a rag-tag such as you!"

Elijah looked silently at the rich man and slowly walked away. As soon as he reached the street outside, he took on the guise of a young royal official. He was dressed in robes

of the finest material, and his carriage was drawn by four horses of rare breed. The moment Joel heard what manner of guest had arrived, he ran out to meet him.

"Unexpected guests are the most welcome of all!" he called out as soon as he reached the door. "Come in, noble sir, and take the place of honor at table next to me. Help yourself to whatever takes your fancy — I am sure you will find something to your taste!"

Joel bowed low to his guest, but when he stood upright again, there in front of him stood the same beggar he had just sent away, and where the horses and carriage had been, there were only the marks of hooves and wheels.

The rich man stood dumbfounded. "What is the meaning of this?" he stammered.

"Nothing much," Elijah replied. "I only wanted to show you how foolish you are. When I presented myself dressed in these beggar's clothes, you did not even offer me a morsel. So I returned dressed as a rich man, and you treated me with honor. You respect the clothes, not the man, though my garments neither eat nor drink. You have no thought for the poor, Joel, and I came to remind you of it. So watch out, lest your pride and meanness bring ruin upon you."

With that Elijah vanished, and Joel, embittered, returned to his guests. He ordered his servants to give the leftovers to the poor and to wayfarers and, thinking he had thus done as the peculiar stranger would have him do, quickly forgot the whole unpleasant incident. He continued to ignore the poor as he had always done.

Some time later Joel went to inspect his fields on Mount Carmel. The melons were just ripening, and he looked forward with pleasure to making a good profit from them. All of a sudden he noticed a strange-looking man coming towards him across the fields. He was dressed in an animal skin, and his hair blew about wildly in the wind. Not knowing that it was Elijah, who had just come out of his cave, Joel shouted at him angrily: "What are you doing in my fields?"

Elijah gave him a look of surprise. "I live on Mount Carmel," he said, "and I have to get down from it somehow. But I am glad I have met you. You are the owner of these fields, and I am hungry and thirsty. Give me one of your melons, I beg of you, that I may refresh myself."

Joel was just about to give the fellow a piece of his mind for his impudence, when it occurred to him to make fun of Elijah instead. With a malicious grin, he said: "You look like a good–for–nothing, and you don't even know food when you see it. Those are not melons lying in my fields, but stones that have been left there."

Elijah nodded his head, then said sadly, "I warned you, Joel, but you have not improved your ways. May God, therefore, make your words come true."

Elijah had scarcely finished speaking when all the melons in Joel's fields turned into stones. In one blow he lost his greatest riches, and from that day forth good fortune abandoned him. His business went from bad to worse, and his property shrank further and further, until the rich man ended up just as Elijah had foretold: penniless and destitute. The remains of his melons, cursed by Elijah, can be seen on the slopes of Mount Carmel to this day. Those smooth, round stones recall the justice of the prophet Elijah, and their hardness is a lesson to all those who are hard of heart.

The Leg from the Table
of the Just

Many, many centuries ago, there lived in the Holy Land a certain merchant. He was a pious man, zealous in prayer and in good deeds, and God had endowed him with great riches. By prudence and diligence he increased his portion daily, but he did not forget the poor, and the more generous he was to those who needed his help, the more Providence favored him.

It is said, however, that while God turns His face away from the wanton, to the just He sends temptation. So the merchant was tempted. Every day he saw so much money and gold, receiving caravans laden with goods, that in the end his riches and renown turned his head. No one noticed it, for he gave alms liberally, paid for physicians for the poor, and donated money to build synagogues; but greed had taken root deep in his heart. At his prayers, morning, afternoon and evening, he beseeched God to send him a great treasure. The merchant had become accustomed to God's favor, and he was sure that his good fortune would continue. On the way to the synagogue or to do business, in the city or out of it, he never took his eyes off the ground, never thought of anything else but that no treasure might escape his gaze.

Early one morning the merchant was visited by an old man dressed in a cloak such as that worn by the Bedouin. "What can I do for you?" the owner of the shop asked him.

"I need nothing," replied the old man. "But I bring you a message. Your prayers have been answered. You will find a golden treasure this very day."

The merchant was overjoyed. He pondered how he might reward the messenger for this good news, but before he could think of anything, the old man had vanished. He was gone as swiftly as he had appeared, leaving the merchant wondering whether he had indeed spoken to someone, or just imagined it.

That evening he returned to his shop full of anticipation. He carefully scrutinized every yard of his route, but noticed nothing out of the ordinary. Then all at once, when he was almost home, he stumbled over something. When he looked down at the ground, he could not believe his eyes. In a place where there had been nothing at all a moment before lay a huge piece of gold in the shape of a table-leg. With trembling hands the merchant picked up the treasure. It was so heavy he could scarcely lift it. "God has truly heard my prayer!" he rejoiced. He quickly looked all about him, and when he was sure no one had seen him, he carried the golden leg off to a secret spot and concealed it carefully.

That night the merchant could not sleep. He was worried in case someone had seen him with the gold, and he turned over and over in his head the question of how much his treasure was worth, and what he might buy with it. The next morning, filled with impatience, he sought out the biggest goldsmith in the city. But he had no sooner told him how big a piece of gold he owned, than the goldsmith raised his eyebrows in suspicion. True, he knew the merchant was a rich man, but he was unable to believe that any ordinary man could come by a piece of gold the size of a table-leg by any honest means.

"The goldsmith thinks I am a thief," the merchant realized with a shock. "It would be better for me to go."

So he quickly took his leave of the goldsmith. He was glad he had got off so lightly, and had not had to explain where he had got his treasure. But what was he to do now? A golden table-leg as such was no good to him, so he decided to go and see a wise man, one who was renowned for his wisdom and integrity far and wide. He set off for the man's house without delay. He told the sage of the treasure he had found, and explained that he could not sell it; but the wise man could not help him.

"I can give you no advice," he told him. "Even if all the goldsmiths you know of were to sell their goods, they could not buy your treasure from you. Only kings and princes could pay you your due. But do you suppose any of them needs one leg from a table?"

The merchant went away sadly, his joy that God had answered his prayer quite gone. As the days passed, he began to feel as if some great invisible burden were weighing him down. He was afraid the goldsmith or the wise man would betray his secret. He realized that a golden table-leg which no one wanted was about as useful to him as a piece of rotten wood. The merchant went to bed dejected, and woke up gloomier than ever.

One evening, low in spirits as usual, he went to bed, and as usual tossed and turned sleeplessly for a long while. When, late in the night, he finally fell asleep, he dreamed he was standing in front of the gates of Paradise. He could hear the beautiful singing of a choir of attendant angels, could smell thousands of wonderful fragrances, each quite different from the others; but he was not permitted to enter the gates. All at once there appeared in front of the merchant an old man, whom he recognized as the one who had visited him in the dress of a Bedouin.

"I am the prophet Elijah," said the old man, pleasantly. "Follow me, please."

Elijah took the merchant into Paradise and led him to a row of golden tables, where the just sat feasting on golden chairs. All the tables had three legs, except for one at which no one was sitting, which was swaying about on two.

"This is the table," said Elijah, turning to the merchant, "at which you are to eat in the world to come."

"But why has my table only two legs, when the others have three?" the merchant inquired with surprise.

"Because you received one of the legs during your life on earth," the prophet replied.

The merchant awoke early the next morning, and without washing or eating or drink-

ing hurried to the synagogue. "Dear God," he begged, "take back the golden leg from the table of the just. I want no more treasures — I will give away all I own to the poor. Only do not leave me what does not belong to me. I know I have sinned, but what of the other just men? They do not deserve to eat at a table which has one leg missing!"

The merchant prayed all day long, and at night, his heart filled with humility and awe, he went back home. The moment he fell asleep, the prophet Elijah appeared to him again in a dream. Once more he led the merchant into Paradise and showed him the tables where the just sat and ate, including the one which had had a leg missing the night before. But this time the table stood firm, resting on three legs like all the others.

In the morning the merchant awoke more refreshed than he had been for a long time. As soon as he had said his prayers he went to the place where he had concealed the golden leg. Search as he would, the treasure was gone. Happy now, he set off back towards his shop, and on the way there he spied, among the buyers in the market-place, the familiar figure of an old man wearing the garb of the Bedouin. The merchant ran towards him, but Elijah merely smiled at him, and before the merchant could get to him, disappeared into the crowd. So thanks to the merchant's repentance the leg from the table of the just returned to Paradise, and it is said that this was a greater miracle than when it came down to earth, since what God gives, He never takes back again.

Travels
with Elijah

Rabbi Joshua ben Levi was known throughout the Holy Land for his learning and his kindness of heart. His words were wise, his deeds were good. Still the great rabbi did not feel happy. He prayed from morning to night, without eating or drinking, beseeching God to hear his plea and allow him to meet the prophet Elijah.

One day at dawn, as Joshua was approaching the synagogue, the prophet appeared before him. "What do you want of me?" he asked the rabbi. "Tell me what you desire."

"The people praise me," Joshua replied, "but I know I still have much to learn. Therefore I long to be able to accompany you on your travels, Elijah. I shall see your pious deeds, the miracles with which you glorify the One God; then I shall indeed be wise."

"What good will it do you to be close to me?" asked Elijah. "You cannot understand what I do with your eyes alone; you are sure to ask me questions, and that will make our journey tiresome."

"I promise to ask nothing!" Joshua replied. "I will only watch what you do — that is all I ask."

"Very well," said Elijah, "come with me. But if you are not able to remain silent, if you ask the reasons for my actions, then we shall part at once."

Joshua agreed, and the two men soon set off on their travels together. They walked and walked, until darkness fell and they came upon the house of a poor man. The little house was barely standing, and starlight shone in through the cracks in its roof; the old man's only possession was a skinny cow tied up in the yard. But he and his wife received the travelers kindly, giving them their own beds to sleep in, and themselves bedding down on a pile of straw in the attic.

The next morning Joshua woke up just in time to hear Elijah at prayer, and almost cried out with dismay. Elijah was asking God to slay the one cow that the poor man owned, and the prophet had scarcely finished his prayers when the animal fell down dead. "What are you doing?" the rabbi asked Elijah reproachfully, unable to restrain himself. "These people are as poor as mice, yet instead of returning their kindness, you only increase their misfortune!"

"I should gladly answer your question," said Elijah, "but we should have to take leave of each other. Remember our agreement."

So Rabbi Joshua asked no more questions, and followed the prophet in silence as they set off on their travels again. That evening the pair of them reached the home of a rich man. His house had many beautifully furnished rooms, and the savor of roast meat came wafting from his kitchen, but Elijah and Joshua were offered neither food nor shelter. The travelers slept in the courtyard, and in the morning prepared to set off again with empty stomachs. Beside the rich man's house there stood a broken-down wall, which the master of the house was about to repair. He was making ready for the work, when Elijah knelt down to pray, and there instead of rubble stood a brand new wall.

"What sort of justice is this?" thought Joshua. "A miser like him, and Elijah must help him!" But he did not say a word; closing his lips tight, with an embittered frown he set off after the prophet. That day the travelers reached a large synagogue. Everything in it was of gold and silver, and places in the pews were divided among the faithful according to the office each of them held. The most respected citizens had comfortable seats with cushions, while the others had narrower ones without cushions. When Elijah and Joshua entered, there were three richly dressed men standing inside.

"Beggars again," said one of them, inclining his head towards the newcomers without even looking at them. "Who's going to feed them?"

"A piece of stale bread and a little water is good enough for the likes of them," said the second man.

The three rich men left at once, but none of them returned with food, and Elijah and Joshua spent a cold night on the synagogue floor. The next morning the three men came to pray, and Elijah said to them: "God grant that you all become elders of the community!"

It was all Rabbi Joshua could do to contain his indignation. "How can Elijah show such kindness to men who are more deserving of punishment?" he thought. "Can anyone witness such behavior without saying a word?" Joshua had already taken breath to ask Elijah for an explanation, but at the last moment he recalled the promise he had made to the prophet. He therefore shook his head at Elijah's treatment of the men, and set off beside him sadder than ever.

As the sun was setting, the two men reached another town. They had scarcely entered its streets when the people began to greet them, everyone trying to persuade Elijah and Joshua to accept their hospitality. In the end the travelers spent the night in the finest of the houses and were brought choice food and drink. In the morning the most eminent citizens of the town came to take their leave of the visitors. The prophet did not even mention their warm welcome, and wished them only: "God grant that one of you become an elder of the community!"

This time Rabbi Joshua was unable to control himself. "Elijah!" he cried angrily, "I wished to stay with you as long as possible, but I can be silent no longer. Tell me why you reward evil and not good. I do not understand you at all, and I should rather part from you than suffer your behavior any longer!"

"As you wish," said the prophet kindly. "Then I shall tell you what you ask to know, and we shall part. Know you, Joshua, that instead of the poor man's cow, his wife was to have died that day. The Angel of Death was in the house, so I begged God to take the life of the beast instead. God granted my plea, so the good man may live with his wife for many years to come. For the rich man who treated us with indifference, I built a wall. In the foundations of that wall there was a great treasure, and if he were to have done the work himself he would surely have found it. The men in the fine synagogue did not know what hospitality is, so I wished they might all be made elders of the community. They will agree on nothing, argue among themselves, and bring the town to ruin with their discord. It is not for nothing that it is said that a ship with many helmsmen will end up on the bottom, but that a single helmsman will bring the vessel safely home. That is also why I wished that there might be only one elder among the citizens who were so kind to us."

When Elijah had finished speaking, he embraced Rabbi Joshua and said quietly, "You wished to learn greater wisdom from me, but there is only one thing which is important: if you come across a godless man who prospers, and a just man who lives in tribulation, do not be deceived. You have seen that God is just, and that His judgement reaches further than the vision of man. Who can advise God what to do?"

When he had said these words, Elijah gave Joshua his blessing, and before the rabbi knew what was happening he had vanished from sight.

The Gift
of the Prophet Elijah

At the time when the prophet Elijah, bene-
factor of Israel, wandered the Holy Land, there lived not far from Jerusalem a poor
man and his family. All they had in the world was a small field and a tumbledown cottage whose walls shook with every gust of wind. There was not much room inside it,
and it seemed to grow smaller all the time, for year by year the cries of a new baby were
heard there. The man already had eight children and, though he toiled in his field from
dawn till dusk, he did not manage to earn enough so that his family would not have
to go to bed hungry.

One day the man was ploughing his field. The work was hard, for the plough kept
running into stones, and by the time the sun had reached its zenith only a narrow strip
of the field was ploughed. The man was sadly considering how little he had done when
the prophet Elijah suddenly appeared in front of him in the guise of an old Arab.

"Peace be with you," he greeted the farmer. "Heaven has ordained that seven years
of good fortune shall be your lot. Will you have them now, or at the end of your life?"

The man had no idea who it was who spoke to him. Thinking the Arab was an evil
sorcerer, he turned on him angrily, saying, "Be off with you, magician, and leave me in
peace! I have enough troubles without you!"

So Elijah went away, but the next day he returned. "Peace be with you, farmer,"
he said. "Seven years of good fortune have been allotted you. Do you want them now,
or at the end of your life?"

The man drove the mysterious Arab away a second time, also; but Elijah came back
again on the third day. "I want nothing more of you," he assured the farmer, "than
the answer to a single question: do you want your seven years of good fortune now,
or at the end of your life?"

This time it did not seem to the farmer that the Arab wished him harm, but he hesitated to answer. "I have always asked my wife's advice on everything," he said to Elijah
in the end. "I should like to ask her opinion this time as well."

Elijah agreed, so the man hurried home to tell his wife about his strange visitor. "If
it is our lot to live better," said his wife, "then it were better so at once. We could hardly
be worse off than we are now, and who knows what the future will bring."

The man returned to the field and told Elijah what his wife had said. "It shall be as you desire," the prophet told him. "You shall become rich this very day; but remember that your good fortune is certain only for seven years. After that I shall visit you once more."

That evening, when the farmer arrived home, he saw at once that the old Arab's words had not been idle. The children showed him a huge lump of gold they had found buried in the garden, and the man and his wife thanked God for His help. As soon as the children had been put to bed, the two of them sat down at the table to decide what to do with their wealth.

"Let us move from here," the farmer suggested, "and buy a big house in the city. We shall have servants and fine horses, and forget all about our poverty."

"But what shall we do in seven years?" his wife asked. "When we have spent the money we receive for the gold, we shall be as poor as ever. No, husband: let us arrange things quite differently. Let's buy the children some proper clothes, and see to it that they do not go hungry. Otherwise we'll end up just as before. Let's get better implements and a field with more fertile soil, and with God's grace we may earn enough to want for nothing until we die. Let us put aside what is left of the money, and use it to help those who are in need, since we have not been abandoned at our time of need."

The farmer took his wife's advice, and soon realized how prudent she was. Their new field brought them a crop many times larger than they had had before. With the profits from their grain the man bought sheep and cattle, so he was able to trade in wool and sell milk and cheese. All who were hungry or had no roof over their heads knew they could always come to him and find his door open. And the more generous he was to the needy, the more his own portion grew.

So the years passed by. Seven years to the day after good fortune had smiled upon the farmer, the prophet Elijah kept his promise. Dressed as an old Arab, he visited the old man in his field, and said: "The seven years are up. Give me back what is left of the treasure."

"I accepted your gift on the advice of my wife," the man replied, "and I can return it only with her consent. Let me, I pray you, tell her of your request."

Elijah had no objection, so the man went home. When his wife had heard what he had to say, she answered: "Tell your benefactor that we have saved up by our own work a sum equal to what we received for the treasure. We can therefore return the whole amount, and we still shall not want."

The man ran back to the field and told the prophet what his wife had said. When Elijah heard these words, he rejoiced, gave the man his blessing, and said: "Be glad that you have a wife so wise. I wanted to give the treasure to one who would use it better than you, but now I see that I should not find such a one. So keep my gift, and add it to what you have saved, and use all the money as prudently as you have till now."

Elijah took his leave of the farmer and he and his wife and children had good fortune for the rest of their lives.

All Is
for the Best

Many a long year ago there lived in the Holy Land a learned man called Rabbi Nachman. Whatever happened, whether fortune was kind or unkind, whether people grew richer or poorer, fell sick or were cured, the rabbi would always say the same thing: "*Gam zu letova*" — "that, too, is for the best". For this reason he was given the nickname Gamzu, and in time no one ever called him anything else. But almost nobody knew the wisdom of the rabbi's words, or what experience had taught them to him.

When Gamzu was a young man, just after his marriage, he set out to visit his father-in-law, taking with him a number of gifts. Rabbi Nachman started his journey with three donkeys. One was loaded with roast meat, done to a turn, and crisply baked biscuits, the second with leather bottles filled with choice wine, and the third with figs, dates, apples, pears and raisins. Gamzu walked on and on till midday, when, with the sun at its hottest, he spied a tall tree under which an old man was resting. The stranger was dressed in rags; his feet were torn and bleeding, and he could scarcely move for exhaustion.

"My good man," he called out to the rabbi, with a great effort. "I cannot take another step for hunger. Give me something to eat, I beg of you."

"Wait a moment," the rabbi answered. "I have been traveling since daybreak: first I must relieve the donkeys. As soon as I have unloaded their packs I will give you bread, meat, wine and fruit."

Gamzu led the donkeys into the shade of a tree and set to work, but suddenly the other man's head slumped, and his soul left his body.

"What have I done!" cried the rabbi in horror. "If only I had helped him right away, instead of just saying I would, the poor fellow might still be alive. His death is on my conscience, and no punishment is too great for me. May my eyes, which did not take pity on this man, cease to see. May my hands, which did not give him food, be paralysed. May my legs, which did not run to help him at once, be shortened. And may my soul find no peace until my whole body is covered with ulcers!"

From the day he met that unfortunate traveler, Rabbi Nachman changed completely. He always carried money in his hand, so that no beggar would have to wait for his alms. He looked after the poor, and his generosity and learning won him great acclaim. "*Gam zu letova,*" the rabbi would say. "Because my neglect killed a man, I learned to lessen human misery. If it were not for that, I should never have understood a single book of Holy Writ."

But as he grew older, Nachman was afflicted by all the ills he had once wished upon himself. He went blind, and walked on crutches; his hands were palsied, and his skin covered with an unsightly rash. "Is that, too, to the good?" his pupils asked him.

"It is," Rabbi Gamzu replied. "I know what I have done to deserve my suffering, and who knows, my pain may save others tears."

The unfortunate rabbi had no idea how soon his words were to come true. For he lived at a time when life was hard for the Jews. They were ruled over by the Romans, and the Emperor Hadrian had a particular dislike for them. One day, an old Jew happened to pass him in the street. "Peace be with you, Caesar," he greeted the Emperor respectfully. But Hadrian flew into a rage. "What impudence is this?" he cried. "That Jew greets me as if I were a friend of his!" He gave the order, and the old man was executed. The next day another Jew passed Hadrian. Knowing what had happened to his fellow, he did not greet the Emperor. But Hadrian was enraged again. "How dare you not show your respect for me!" he shrieked at the unfortunate man. "Am I not worth your greeting me?" He gave the order, and another Jew was executed.

The Jews in the Roman Empire were seized with fear and dismay. "If Caesar's hatred for us is so great," they lamented, "he will surely destroy us all. If we do not find a way to appease him, it will be the end of us!" So the wisest of the rabbis put their heads together to decide what to do; but it was only after long deliberation that they resolved to send the Emperor a splendid jewel. The Jews knew that he adored gold and precious gems, and felt sure that their rare gift would appease Hadrian. The only remaining question was who should take it to the all-powerful ruler.

"It should be somebody young and handsome," said some of the rabbis, "so he won't annoy Caesar."

"On the contrary," said others, "an old man would be better for such a task. Gray hair commands respect."

In the end Gamzu rose to address the gathering. "No one knows what sort of a mood Caesar will be in," he said. "Perhaps he will want to see a young man, perhaps an old one. Only one thing is certain. The envoy should be one who has nothing to lose. And I ask you: is there any in Israel more wretched than I?"

At these words the rabbis gave Nachman their blessing, and handed him the inlaid casket containing the jewel for the Emperor Hadrian. Then all the Jews prayed for his safety. Early the next morning Gamzu set out on his journey.

The rabbi trekked all day without rest, and it was already dark when he reached an inn on the outskirts of a small town. The innkeeper and his wife were hospitality itself: they willingly offered Nachman a bed for the night and gave him good food and drink, but their smiles were only a mask for their evil intentions. As soon as Gamzu had fallen asleep, the innkeeper turned to his wife and said: "Did you see the beautiful inlaid casket that old Jew was carrying? There is surely some treasure in it!"

"We shall soon see," replied his wife. She crept quietly into the room where Rabbi Nachman was sleeping, and brought out the casket. When the innkeeper opened it and saw the wonderful jewel it contained, his head spun with excitement. He quickly told his wife to put a little earth from the garden into the casket, and to put it back where she had found it. She did as he told her, and the same night he buried the jewel in his cellar so that no one would find it.

At dawn Gamzu prepared to continue his journey. The innkeeper thought that the blind rabbi would not notice that the jewel was missing, but Nachman only had to touch the casket to know what had happened. Nonetheless, he was not angry with the innkeeper, and did not say a word of reproach to him. "*Gam zu letova*" was all he said, as was his wont. "That, too, is for the best." And with faith in God's help he set off for Rome.

After a long and arduous journey, Gamzu stood at last before the Emperor Hadrian. The rabbi handed over to him a conciliatory letter written in the name of the whole Jewish people, and with it the inlaid casket. When Hadrian read that the Jews were sending him a rare gift, he opened the casket curiously; but at once his brow darkened.

"What kind of prank is this?" he cried, menacingly. "Will the Jews mock me, that they send me ordinary soil? Not even the greatest treasure on earth could reconcile me with them, and now the dogs would laugh at me! I shall have all the Jews put to death!" he ranted. "Every last one of them, that they may never again hold Caesar in contempt!"

The Emperor signaled to the guard to take Gamzu off for execution; but the soldiers had scarcely bound the rabbi's hands when into the chamber stepped the prophet Elijah, disguised as one of Caesar's counselors. "Hadrian," Elijah said soothingly, "do not allow your wrath to carry you away. Perhaps the earth which Gamzu has brought you is not so ordinary. Is it not well-known that Abraham, forefather of the Jews, defeated his enemies with the aid of miraculous earth? It turned into spears, slingstones and battering rams which opened the strongest gates; there was not a fortress which could resist them."

Hadrian stopped short: his legions were constantly at war. There was always some mutiny or other among his troops, and there was nothing he, ruler of the Roman Empire, could wish for more than a weapon which would guarantee victory. He therefore gave orders that Gamzu's life should be spared until the army had tested the properties of the earth he had brought. Within a week the first reports were arriving, and Hadrian did not conceal his enthusiasm. When Rabbi Nachman's earth was thrown at a fortress which the Romans had besieged in vain for many months, the walls split asunder, the enemy troops fell down dead, and Caesar's legions won an easy victory. Hadrian let the rabbi go at once, promising never to harm the Jews again, and rewarding him with much gold, silver and precious stones.

Gamzu returned to Jerusalem with a light heart. His nation had been saved, and in the end the greed of the innkeeper and his wife who had robbed him on the way to Rome had been to the Jews' advantage. Gamzu therefore did not forget to visit the inn on his way back. He recounted to the amazement of the innkeeper how successful he had been in Rome, how pleased Caesar had been with the earth, and how graciously he had been rewarded for it.

The innkeeper could have burst with envy. The moment the rabbi left, he called his laborers and had them dig up the whole of his garden. Then, with several wagonloads of earth, he set off for Rome. An appetite for riches drove the innkeeper on; he could not wait to be received by the Emperor, and to reap his reward. At long last he stood before Hadrian. "Caesar," he said with a low bow, "the wonderful earth of Rabbi Nachman was from my garden. Look out of the window at my wagons: all that is for you."

The Emperor looked searchingly at his visitor. "There is something strange here," he thought. "If the innkeeper had marvelous earth, he would hardly give it to Rabbi Nachman. Most likely this fellow is a fine old swindler." Nonetheless, Hadrian had the earth tested to see what it could do. It was found to be ordinary soil, the same as any other, and the miracle by which the prophet Elijah helped Rabbi Nachman was not repeated. The innkeeper had no choice but to admit the theft of the jewel which was intended for Hadrian. The unfortunate fellow wept and beseeched the Emperor for mercy, but he did not escape his just punishment. He paid for his wicked deed, and his wife, too, soon lost all she had gained by her theft. She had to return the jewel which was buried in the cellar to the Jews, who remembered with gratitude the prophet Elijah, Rabbi Nachman, and his saying "*Gam zu letova*".

The Ungrateful Deer

Some hunters went out in pursuit of deer. As they approached a large grove, they spotted a splendid deer at its edge. They set off after him at once, but he ran into the grove and hid among the bushes. The hunters searched for him in vain; they looked all about them, but in the end went away disappointed.

As soon as the deer saw that his pursuers were going home, he began to eat the leaves which had concealed him from danger. The leaves began to sigh. "What is the matter?" asked the trees. "Why do you sigh so sadly? Are you unhappy that you are being eaten by the deer?"

"That is not the reason we grieve," the leaves replied. "We are sorry for the deer who is eating us. The poor creature does not know that the hunters will soon find him."

But the deer took no notice of the leaves. He ate them one by one, as if their cover had not saved his life, and before long his body could be seen among the bushes. The strange rustling in the grove attracted one of the hunters. He looked to see where it was coming from, and saw the deer among the stripped bushes. The hunter quickly called his companions, and the deer was shot.

"It is the punishment I deserve!" cried the deer as he died. "I forgot the hospitality of the leaves, and repaid their good deed with a bad one. How could I escape misfortune?"

The Head and the Tail

The snake's tail complained to the head one day: "Why should I have to follow you around all the time? No one made you my master, and indeed I know no reason why I should go behind you like your servant. From now on all will be different. I shall go in front, and you will follow me!" The head did not object, so the body set off after the tail. But, having no eyes, the tail could not avoid the obstacles it met. It bumped into sharp stones, got entangled in thorns and thistles, splashed through puddles, and finally burned itself in a fire. If the head had not led the body out of the fire, the whole snake would have died in the flames.

Just as the tail wanted to lead the head, so it is when an inexperienced young man wants to make decisions instead of a wise old man. As it is written: if the old tell you to destroy and the young to build, then destroy, and do not build; for old men's destruction is building, and young men's building destruction.

THE FOURTH
LIGHT

The Mighty Rulers and Famous Rabbis Living in the Holy Land during the Roman Occupation

Alexander's Lesson

The Macedonian king, Alexander the Great, was the greatest conqueror the world has ever known. He defeated all his enemies, and no one could resist his hosts. The rulers of all countries trembled at his name, and the fame of his invincibility and courage spread the world over.

One day Alexander took a great army to subjugate the Holy Land and Jerusalem. His troops looked forward to the campaign, thinking they would put the Jews to the sword and plunder their land, but Alexander decided otherwise. When a file of white-robed priests came out from the gates of Jerusalem to meet him, led by the high priest, whose headband contained a golden tablet inscribed with the name of God, Alexander fell to his knees, praised the one God, and was the first to greet the high priest. Then he permitted the Jews to retain all their customs, attacking neither their honor nor their religion. When the astonished captains, accustomed to rich spoils, demanded an explanation, Alexander said, "I once saw in a dream a man just like the Jewish high priest. He gave me courage, prophesied that my expeditions would end in success. His words came true, which is why I will not allow the Jews to suffer. I shall never cease to respect them, and whenever I am in need of counsel, I shall turn to the elders of this nation."

It was not long before Alexander summoned the elders of the Jews. "I wish to make an expedition to Africa," he told them. "What sort of journey can I expect?"

"Sire," the Jews warned him, "that place is cut off by high black mountains, which swallow up even the rays of the sun. Eternal darkness reigns there, and it is easy to lose one's way. And even if you do reach Africa, you will only be wasting your time there."

"Still, I must go to Africa," Alexander insisted. "What is your advice to me?"

"If you must go," the elders of the Jews told him, "then you should obtain asses from Libya, which do not need to see where they are going. Take a rope, also. Tie one end at the place where you enter the realm of darkness, and keep the other in your hand. Then you will always be able to find your way back."

Alexander did as the Jews had told him. He successfully passed the black mountains and overcame all other obstacles, until he entered Africa with his whole army. Soon he reached the borders of a country inhabited by women. Alexander declared war on them at once, but they sent him a message in reply: "Do not be foolish, O king; why should you enter into a war which will bring you nothing? If you kill us, you will bring disdain upon yourself; people will speak of 'Alexander, who conquered mere women'. If we kill you, you will be mocked in your grave. People will say 'a conqueror such as he, and see how he ended up'."

Alexander admitted the truth of what the women said, and asked to be allowed to visit their land at least. The women agreed, and held a great banquet in his honor. Alexander was given the place of honor, and the servants began to fetch the first courses. The Macedonian king was very hungry, and looked forward to the savor of exotic dishes, but to his astonishment all the foods were of pure gold.

"What is the meaning of this?" Alexander asked in surprise. "Is it possible to eat gold? Give me some dry bread, that my stomach may stop rumbling."

"We had no idea you would be satisfied with ordinary bread," the women replied. "But if that is all you ask, why did you bother to come all this way? Had you not bread enough at home?"

Alexander realized that once again he did not know how to reply, and left in shame. "What a fool I was, I, Alexander, to come to Africa, only to be told what to do by women," he wrote on the gate of the unconquered city. And he said to himself: "Behold, the Jews were right again. Truly it was a waste of time for me to come to Africa."

On the way home Alexander and his soldiers paused beside a small river. He was tired, and his whole body ached from the long journey. When he had slept awhile, the king took some dried fish out of his satchel. He dipped them in the water to wash the salt off them, but the moment the fish were beneath the surface, their bodies came to life, and one after another they slipped out of Alexander's hand and swam away.

"What miraculous water this is!" the king said to himself. He sniffed its pleasant odor, and with every breath it seemed that fresh blood surged through his veins. In the end he could not resist washing his face in the river. At that instant his eyes shone, his weariness left him, and Alexander felt more at peace than ever before.

"I have seen many things," the king said to himself, "but never before have I known such bliss. I would rather lose all the lands I have conquered than not see the source of this marvelous river, and the country which surrounds it!" Then he ordered his troops to wait for him, and set off upstream alone.

Alexander found himself at the foot of tall cliffs. He walked along narrow defiles, forced his way through thick bushes, until the water in the river began to get shallower, and he came across a huge wall from which the stream sprang. He looked for a gate, but wherever he turned he saw only the moss-covered wall, seeming to stretch endlessly. The king walked up and down, bewildered, and when he could not find the merest crevice, he struck the wall several times and called out: "I, Alexander, will enter! The whole world obeys my command; all the nations of the earth pay tribute to me. So whoever is within these walls, let him open and let me in, or he shall know my wrath!"

Alexander had scarcely finished these words when a piece of moss fell from the wall in front of him, and a gate appeared. But no one opened it, and all around there was a silence like that of the grave. Then, suddenly, a loud voice roared in the king's ears:

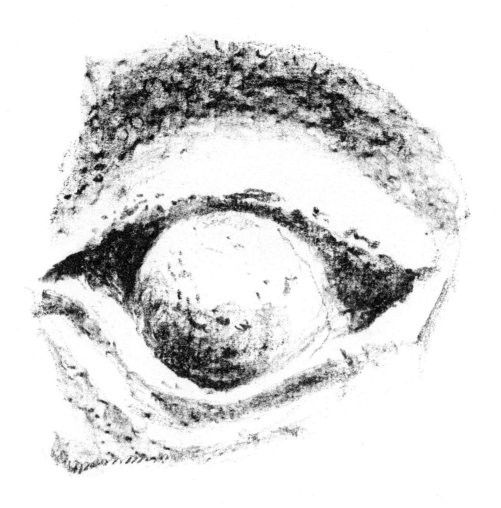

"Alexander, you stand before the gates of Paradise. Put aside your threats, and examine your conscience. Only the just may enter God's house!"

But Alexander was not overawed. "If I am truly standing before the gates of Paradise," he called out, "then I should like to take away something to remind me of it."

When he had spoken these words, the gate opened a crack, and a polished stone in the shape of a human eye fell at his feet. "Here is the gift you desire," the roaring voice said. "Try to understand it, and be grateful for God's providence!"

When Alexander returned to his homeland, he summoned all his counselors and wise men, in order that they might reveal to him the mystery of the stone. But the king's advisers merely praised his good fortune and might, and could tell him no more. So Alexander sent to Jerusalem for the Jewish elders. They came prepared to help the king, but even their learning was not enough to explain the mystery. They left Alexander with apologies, and he was as ignorant as ever about his gift from Paradise.

At the time there lived in the town of Susa a certain wise Jew called Papas. He was old, and so ill that if he wanted to leave his house two men had to carry him in a litter. When Papas heard from his friends of Alexander's perplexity over the strange stone, he asked the king for an audience. Alexander had Papas brought to him at once. He expressed his respect for the old man's wisdom, told him of his journey to Africa, and finally showed him the polished stone in the shape of a human eye.

"Mighty lord," Papas told him, "have the stone weighed, I pray you."

"Must it be?" asked Alexander, in surprise. "It surely weighs no more than half a shekel." Something about the strange whims of old men crossed his mind, but he did as Papas asked. He placed the stone on one side of the scales, and a gold weight on the other. But the eye was heavier, and even when Alexander added another piece of gold to the first, and another, and another, the stone was still heavier than them all. Soon the dish of the scales was full, and Alexander had a bigger pair of scales brought. Now he weighed the stone of Paradise not only against gold, but also against silver, pearls and precious stones, and the servants kept bringing more and more chests of treasure.

"You are wasting your efforts, my lord," Papas told him. "Even if you had a pair of scales on which you might place all your palaces and all the riches in them, the stone of Paradise would still outweigh them."

"Explain this to me!" demanded Alexander.

"The eye you have received from Paradise," said Papas, "is the eye of a man made of flesh and blood, which is never sated by riches. It always covets more, and no amount of wealth is enough for it."

"How do you know that this is so?" asked Alexander.

At these words Papas took up a handful of earth and covered the stone eye with it. At that instant the scales tipped suddenly the other way. "You see," Papas told Alexander. "It is enough for a man to die and be covered with soil for all riches to be in vain." Papas looked at the king for a long time. "You are now at the height of your glory, my lord," he told him. "But do not forget the gift of Paradise."

Alexander rewarded Papas richly, and from then till his dying day he kept a rein on his ambition.

Patient
Hillel

Wisdom is not handed down from father to son like houses, fields and riches, and he who does not seek learning will never come by it. That is the way things are, and so when the two great sages of Israel, Shemaya and Avtalion, were teaching in Jerusalem, they were never short of pupils. Their school was attended by both boys and men, but it was not everyone's lot to be able to listen to the holy teaching. The school cost money, and whoever wished to study there had first to pay.

No one was more bothered by this state of affairs than Hillel. He was a man of lowly birth and scant means, but his desire for learning was stronger than anyone's. Hillel rose every morning long before daybreak, so as to find work in the city and earn his usual denarius. As soon as he had it in his hand, he would dash off home with it; he would give half to his wife to buy food, and hurry to the school with the other half. But try as he might, Hillel could not manage to earn a denarius before noon, and he was always late for his lessons. His heart ached for each precious word he lost, but he did not complain, and was grateful that he could spend at least part of the day close to Shemaya and Avtalion.

But one winter's day fortune abandoned Hillel altogether. He did not find work, did not earn his denarius, and the porter would not let him into the school. What was poor Hillel to do? He paced up and down in despair, looking sadly through windows at the fortunate pupils who were hearing the teaching of God. Then an idea occurred to him. He looked around and, seeing that there was no one else about, quickly climbed up onto the roof of the school. There he lay on his stomach, leaning over the edge of the roof to peer in at the schoolroom window, and listen, silent and motionless, to Shemaya and Avtalion's words. The hours crept by, and it began to freeze; soon snow began to fall, but Hillel did not even notice. His heart and mind were engrossed in the secrets which were opening up to him, and in his zeal he felt neither cold nor damp.

The pupils had long since gone home; night was falling, and only Shemaya and Avtalion remained, continuing with their studies alone. At dawn Shemaya raised his eyes from the holy books, and said: "It is usually light by now, but today there is still twilight. What sort of a cloud is that, which is shutting out the light?" The two men went over to the window, and leapt back with a start. Instead of a cloud, they saw the half-frozen Hillel. The learned men hurried to the roof, where they dug out their zealous pupil and took him inside to thaw. After that they told him: "Hillel, your patience deserves rewarding. You may come to school whenever you wish — there is no need for you to pay."

From then on Hillel did not lose a moment's teaching. Shemaya and Avtalion had no pupil more avid, and Hillel's learning grew day by day. Before very long he surpassed even his teachers. Wisdom brought him repute, and repute grew into renown, but it was his charity which won him the affection of his fellow men. He was never angry, never shouted at anyone, and whoever came to see him was received with the same good grace, the same patience.

But there was a certain stranger who did not believe this was so. "There is no man alive who would never lose his temper," he would say, "and Hillel is no exception. I wager four hundred denarii that I can make him angry."

"And I," said his friend, "am willing to wager four hundred that you cannot make him lose his temper."

So the stranger set off for Hillel's house. It was a Friday afternoon, shortly before the start of the Sabbath, which suited the man's purpose very well. He knew that it is a time when Jews are very busy getting ready for the holiday, and he therefore supposed he would disturb Hillel good and proper. Pounding on the door, he cried: "Does Hillel live here? Where is Hillel?"

Those who heard this were astounded. Hillel stood at the head of the wisest men of Israel, and they therefore called him *Nasi* — Prince. This impudent fellow did not even address him as Rabbi. But Hillel was not offended by the foreigner's words, nor did he mind that his visitor was keeping him from his trip to the baths. Opening the door, he asked the man pleasantly: "What do you wish?"

"Just this," the man replied, roughly, "I want to know why the Babylonians have flat heads."

"Well, now," replied Hillel, nodding his head, "that is an interesting question. I daresay it is because their midwives are not too skilful."

The foreigner turned and left without a word of thanks. But before an hour had passed he was back again, shouting louder than ever. "Where is Hillel?"

The stranger's cries interrupted Hillel just as he was putting on his Sabbath clothes. But he quickly threw on a cloak, and opened the door as willingly as before. "What do you wish?" he asked.

"I have another question," the man replied, gruffly. "Tell me why the Thermodanians have bloodshot eyes!"

"That, too, is a good question," replied Hillel, kindly. "It is because they live in a region where there is much fine sand. When the wind blows, the sand gets into people's eyes and makes them bloodshot."

An hour later the foreigner was again standing in front of Hillel's house. "Where is Hillel?" he shouted. "Where is Hillel?"

The man's cries disturbed the meditation which Hillel had entered into in order to await the coming of the Sabbath, but he remained as calm as ever. "What do you wish?" he asked again.

"Tell me why the Africans have flat feet!" demanded the foreigner.

"I am glad you are so eager for knowledge," Hillel replied. "Africans have flat feet because they frequently walk in swamps."

"Hillel," said the foreigner, irritably, "I've got a lot more questions, but I'm afraid to ask, in case you get angry with me."

"Don't be afraid: ask what you like," Hillel replied.

Seeing that he was losing his bet, the stranger began to lose control of himself. "Are you the Hillel the Israelites call Prince?" he shrieked.

"Yes, my friend."

"Then remember this: I am glad there aren't more Jews like you!"

"Why?" asked Hillel, anxiously. "Have I offended you?"

"You have done worse than that!" the man shouted. "I wagered I should make you angry, and I have lost four hundred denarii over you!"

"Thank God that is all," replied Hillel. "It is better to lose one's money than one's patience, for it is easier to earn money than to earn forgiveness."

Hillel bowed to the foreigner, and from then on no one ever doubted his amiability and patience.

Rabbi Chanina ben Dosa

It is written that poverty is to the Jews what the scarlet plume is to a white horse. But even poverty has degrees: there are those who are the poorest of the poor. One such was Rabbi Chanina ben Dosa. He owned nothing, wanted for nothing, and lived for nothing but to teach the holy Torah.

The rabbi's wife, on the other hand, never stopped worrying, and awaited each new day that dawned with fresh anxiety. Chanina spent the whole day with his pupils, but he taught them for nothing except the joy of it, so that there was often no money at home to buy food with, and no food to cook. The worst time of the whole week was the eve of the Sabbath. While the other wives were preparing a holiday supper, making fish ready for cooking and kneading the dough to make bread, in Chanina's house there was silence. The rabbi's wife stood in front of an empty larder, containing nothing but the usual bowl of carob fruit. She worried greatly over their poverty. She worked from morning till night, and when there was nothing else she could do, she tried at least to hide the fact that they were so poor. She would always light a piece of wood in the stove on the eve of the Sabbath, so that the smoke from the chimney might give the impression that there would be a proper festive supper in the rabbi's house, too.

But in the neighboring house there lived a wicked woman. "Where would such as they get the money for fish and flour?" she thought to herself one day. "Chanina's wife is stoking an empty oven, for sure!" Unable to contain her malicious curiosity, the woman went to see for herself.

When the rabbi's wife heard a visitor enter the house, she blushed with shame. Quickly, she hid in the next room, just as her neighbor was coming into the kitchen. The woman looked neither right nor left, but strode straight up to the stove and opened the oven door triumphantly. But instead of an empty baking tray she saw a golden-brown Sabbath loaf, just ready to take out. "Where is everyone?" she cried, confused. "The bread is burning!"

Chanina's wife came into the kitchen. "Here I am," she said calmly, as if she had expected the miracle. "It's not the first time I've ever baked bread, you know." And she smiled at her neighbor, who quickly went away, quite abashed.

That afternoon the rabbi's wife couldn't wait for her husband to get home. "He is

so learned," she thought. "It was surely he who performed the miracle. If only he would do it more often, we should never need to go hungry again."

The moment Chanina appeared in the doorway, his wife ran out to meet him. She wanted to tell him all about it, but the rabbi spoke first. "I did what was necessary," he said. "But do you suppose that I can work miracles on my own? Without the will of God man cannot even lift a finger. Be glad, then, that we have bread for once, and do not be anxious about the morrow."

That evening the rabbi returned from the synagogue accompanied by two travelers. They ate the wonderful bread, spent the whole of the next day at the rabbi's house, and when the holiday was over went their way. But the sun in the heavens had left behind it only a tiny fraction of its long day's trek, when Chanina's wife came running up to him. She held in her hand a hen, and called out, "Look what your guests left at our house! Quickly, go after them, and give them the hen!"

"I do not know where they are from, or where they are going," Chanina replied. "It would be better for us to look after the hen for them until they return to fetch it."

But one day passed, then another, and there was no sign of the two men coming back; the hen started laying eggs. "What shall we do?" asked Chanina's wife. "We have nothing to eat but carob fruit; what if we were to take a couple of the eggs?"

"That we must not," the rabbi said. "The eggs are not ours, for they were laid by a hen which does not belong to us. Leave the hen to hatch her chickens."

Chanina's wife did as she was told, and it was not long before the eggs hatched into chickens. Then the chickens grew up, and began to lay eggs of their own, which also hatched into chickens. Chanina did not have a henhouse, but the chickens and hens were getting more and more numerous, so in the end there was nothing for it but to take them into his own house. "I am sure the men will come soon and take what is theirs," Chanina told his wife. "This way at least I can be sure that none of them will be carried off by a fox."

But time went by, the men did not come, and now there was not only hunger in Chanina's house, but a lack of room as well; wherever you looked there were hens and eggs. "It can't be helped," said the rabbi one day. "We can't all go on living under one roof. We shall sell the hens and the chickens and buy goats; when they return, we shall give the men the goats."

And Chanina did as he had said he would. He bought some goats; but because there was still no sign of the two men, the goats had kids, and before long there was less room in the house than ever. "We shall have to sell the goats," said the rabbi one day. "We shall exchange them for barley, and that way there will be room enough in the house. The important thing is that nothing should be lost, and that the men should receive what is due to them."

So Chanina sold the goats, and with the money he bought barley, which he then planted. That summer he had a fine harvest, and again he planted the barley; the next year the harvest was even better than before. But he went on eating only carob fruit, not having so much as a bowlful of flour ground for him and his wife.

Finally, after three years, the two men who had forgotten the hen returned to Rabbi Chanina's house. The rabbi knew full well who they were. He called his wife, and then said to the men, "Did you not forget a hen here three years ago?"

"You have a good memory, Rabbi," the men replied, surprised. "We did leave a hen here; but we got on well enough without it, and did not miss it."

"Still," said the rabbi, "the hen remains your property, and I am glad that I may return it. Come with me, please."

Chanina beckoned to his guests, and led them to a loft full of grain. "This is your hen," he explained. "It laid eggs, and the eggs grew into hens, which laid new eggs. We sold the hens and bought goats, and when the goats increased in number, I bought barley for them. As you can see, God has blessed your barley, too. Take your grain now, and do not forget that the corn-loft itself was built from a part of the harvest."

His guests looked at each other, perplexed. They stood silently, shuffled their feet: it was clear that they had something on their minds. At last the older man spoke: "Rabbi," he said, moved. "We did not expect a reception such as this, and we must explain something to you. When we were here three years ago, you looked after us as if we were your own sons. We could see that you and your wife lived in poverty, yet you gave us the only bread you had, and offered us your hospitality for the whole of the Sabbath. We wished to repay your kindness, which is why we left a hen in your house. We did so in secret, lest you should in your modesty refuse the hen; nonetheless, it was a gift, and a gift it remains. You will surely understand that we cannot take any of what you offer us. You have acquired this property through your own hard work, and if the hen we left here helped you to do so, then we are truly glad of it."

Now it was Chanina ben Dosa's turn to be surprised. He would not hear of keeping the grain; he begged the men to take some of it at least. But his guests insisted, so Chanina resolved the strange dispute with the decision of a rabbi. "Perhaps," he told the men, "you know the story of the two sheep which had to swim across a river. One of them had beautiful, thick wool, while the second had been shorn. And what happened? The sheep with the splendid fleece got it soaked with water, and was weighed down by it and drowned. The other sheep, which was not so beautiful, and had nothing but her bare body, swam to the other side without trouble. So I, too, would own nothing, and rather than keep the grain, I shall give it to poor travelers. It was your charity to give me the hen, and it shall be mine to get rid of all possessions."

When he had spoken thus, the two travelers bowed low to Chanina, and they spread the word throughout the Holy Land of the rabbi who preferred to live on carob fruit than to keep anything for himself.

Rabbi Ishmael
and the Dream-Teller

Some pupils are like funnels: what goes in at one end comes out at the other. But Ishmael, son of the famous man of learning Yossi Hagalili, was more like a sponge. A sponge soaks everything up, and Ishmael forgot nothing of what he was taught. When he grew up he became a rabbi, and there were few who could match his learning. Pupils came from far and wide to hear his teaching, and they respected their master more than their own fathers.

But one year something went wrong. The rabbi had fewer pupils every day, and those that remained paid little attention to the holy teaching. Ishmael could not understand this sudden change. "Either my learning has left me, or someone is taking away my pupils," he said to himself in the end. So he went to the market and listened to what people were saying, and it was not long before he knew just what was going on.

"Have you heard about the marvelous Samaritan?" a butcher was saying. "He can interpret any dream!"

"It's true!" cried one of his customers, taking up the theme at once. "All he needs is a couple of words, and he'll foretell you the future."

The rabbi did not wait to hear more. He hurried to the place where the Samaritan had put up his tent, and Ishmael was not surprised to see nearly all his pupils inside. They were listening to the Samaritan's words as devoutly as if they came out of the mouth of one of the prophets, and they hardly noticed their rabbi.

"What do you want?" the Samaritan asked Ishmael.

"I have heard you can foretell the future," Ishmael replied, "and I have come to see for myself."

"You are lucky," said the Samaritan, importantly. "There are four people just awaiting an audience." The Samaritan gave a sign, and an old man entered the tent. He bowed, and said: "I saw in a dream that I had three eyes. What does this mean?"

"Nothing more nor less," replied the Samaritan, "than that your eyesight will improve. You will see like a hawk."

"What is that you are saying?" the rabbi joined in. "Why, this man has red eyes. He is surely a baker, and the third eye in his dream is the glowing oven in which he bakes his bread."

"Indeed I am a baker," the man gasped in surprise, "and I gaze into the fire every day. The flames of the oven burn my eyes, and my sight is getting worse day by day."

The Samaritan frowned, gave the baker back the money he had received from him, and had the next man called in. A merchant entered the tent. "I dreamed I had four ears," he said. "Is that a good omen or a bad one?"

"A good one," the Samaritan assured him. "You will become famous the world over."

Rabbi Ishmael shook his head. "You are wrong again, Samaritan. A man sees in his dreams only what is in his heart. If you look outside the tent you will see the merchant's donkey. He is constantly looking at the creature's ears, so in his dream he saw them on his own head."

The Samaritan frowned more than ever, and gave the merchant his money back. Soon a third man had come in. "Samaritan," he said, "the moment I fell asleep yesterday, a book with twenty-four pages appeared to me. How am I to explain that?"

"Do not worry," the Samaritan told him. "You are a merchant, and what you saw was your account book."

Ishmael laughed out loud. "How could that poor fellow be a merchant?" he cried. "Why, his clothes are patched all over!"

Like it or not, the Samaritan had to give the third man his money back like the other two. He scowled angrily at Ishmael, but the fourth man had come into the tent. "I had a very strange dream," he told the Samaritan. "I met a lot of people, and they were all pointing their fingers at me."

"That," said the Samaritan, "means that you will be highly esteemed. When you go through the town, people will greet you as their teacher and counselor."

This time Rabbi Ishmael could contain himself no longer. "Is that the kind of talk you come to hear?" he shouted at his pupils. "Why, this man for whom the Samaritan foretells esteem is already considered a fool! Because of his dreams he let the work on his harvest fall behind, and all his wheat was soaked in the field!"

His pupils hung their heads guiltily, and set out with Rabbi Ishmael to see the farmer's field. Their teacher had told the truth. Rain had ruined all the man's grain, and he was a laughing stock.

From the time the rabbi visited him, the Samaritan had a bad time of it. Nobody was interested in his explanations of their dreams, and he pondered in vain how he might win back his customers. At last he had an idea. "Ishmael made a liar of me," he said to himself, "and turned them all against me. But if I can show that he cannot tell the meaning of dreams, people will come back to me."

The Samaritan called one of his followers and said to him: "Go to Ishmael, and ask him to explain some dream you have made up. Whatever he tells you, you will say it is wrong. Then we shall say the rabbi is a fraud, and those he turned away from me will come back again."

The Samaritan's accomplice set off at once. He found the rabbi, asked him to explain his dream, and told him: "I dreamed I saw four cedars, four carob trees, and a bale of straw, on which I was lying. What does this mean?"

Rabbi Ishmael looked at the man with suspicion. "A truly interesting dream," he said. "It is only a pity that you have made it all up. But I like riddles, and I shall give you an answer just the same. The four cedars are the four legs of your bed. The four carob trees are its four sides. The bale is the straw on which you lie, and you are the ass which lies on it!"

When the lying Samaritan heard how his friend had got on, he quickly struck his tent and hurried off to find a place where people did not know him. Rabbi Ishmael went on teaching his pupils as before, and they never allowed themselves to be deceived by dream-tellers again.

Simeon
ben Yohai

Whoever wishes to understand the holy book of the Jews, the Torah, must be like water. Why like water? Because water does not stay up in the heights of the mountains, but flows down to people. Rabbi Simeon ben Yohai was just such a man. He knew many things, but he did not keep his learning to himself: he wrote books of wisdom, and offered his help to all who needed it. But not even Rabbi Simeon was born with wisdom. He had to acquire his learning, and the price he paid for it was no small one. It happened like this.

One day Rabbi Simeon ben Yohai was discussing the holy teaching with his friend Rabbi Yossi. At that time the Jews had a hard life. The Roman occupation forced them to keep some of their laws secretly, and so when the rabbis saw Judah ben Gerim approaching, they fell silent. They knew only too well that Judah had exchanged his faith in the One God for the friendship and rewards of the Romans, and they did not trust him at all. Judah, as usual, began at once to praise the rule of the Romans. He described their buildings with enthusiasm, and waxed lyrical about their customs and their wise government; but Simeon ben Yohai interrupted him. "You should be ashamed of yourself, Judah," he said. "Instead of preserving the heritage of our forefathers, you extol those who spill Jewish blood. Whatever the Romans do, they do for their own good; but to us they have brought only tears and grief."

Before the sun had set the Roman governor had word of the conversation. "What impudence!" he cried, beside himself with anger. "Simeon ben Yohai has offended against the dignity of the Empire, and I sentence him to death. Let sentence be executed immediately!"

The ruler of the city sent guards to arrest the rabbi at once, but Simeon did not wait for his executioners. He took his son, Rabbi Eleazar, and the two of them hid in an abandoned synagogue. But the soldiers began to search from street to street and from house to house, and the two of them were obliged to slip away one night and hide in the nearby mountains. There they took refuge in a cave, and, search as they might, the Romans could find no trace of them. It was as if the ground had opened up to swallow Simeon and Eleazar.

Simeon ben Yohai and his son had managed to save their lives, but it was not the end of their troubles. In the synagogue a good woman had brought them bread and water every day. But what were they to eat here, among the rocks, far away from other men? The first night in the cave Rabbi Simeon went to sleep with a heavy heart. When he woke up, however, he could not believe his eyes. While he and his son had slept, a huge carob tree had grown in the cave, and a spring of water was pouring out of the rock, so that the two men had both food and drink. Now Rabbi Simeon was afraid of nothing. He and his son took off their clothes, buried themselves up to their necks in sand, and studied the Torah together. They put on their clothes only when the hour of prayer came. Then they took off their clothes again and continued to study God's teaching, buried in the sand. This went on day after day and year after year, until Rabbi Simeon learned in a dream that they were no longer in danger, because the Roman governor had died. For a whole twelve years Simeon ben Yohai and his son Eleazar had not seen the light of day. When they finally left their cave, their knowledge was so great that they had to take care not to set fire to the ground with the brilliance of their gaze. They wandered throughout the Holy Land, and everywhere the people greeted them as envoys of wisdom, men who were just and devoted to their nation.

One day a man and his wife from the town of Sidon came to see Simeon ben Yohai. The woman's eyes were red from crying, and the man, too, was quite downcast. "What has happened to you?" Simeon asked them. "Perhaps I can help."

"That is why we came to see you," the man replied. "But, Rabbi, you must believe us that we would rather get by without your help." The visitor fell silent for a while, then continued in a shaky voice. "My wife and I have been married for ten years, and all that time we have lived in harmony and love. But God has not granted us children, and what happiness is there without the laughter of children? Since we only wish the best for each other, we have decided to part. Perhaps one of us at least will have the good fortune to beget children; thus we ask you to divorce us."

"I shall do as you ask," said the rabbi. "But first you should hold a great feast, as you did for your wedding. It was then that your paths were united, so let them part again in the same manner. Then come back to me, and I shall divorce you according to the law of Israel."

The couple thanked Simeon, and they were about to leave when the rabbi went up to the man and whispered something in his ear, quietly, so that the wife might not hear. "Take your leave of her as is befitting. Before going to bed, offer your wife the most precious thing she can find in your house." The man nodded his understanding, and in a few moments the door had closed behind the pair of them.

As soon as the husband and wife got home, they began to prepare the feast. The woman cooked all manner of tasty dishes and the man bought wine, and together they invited musicians and many guests. The celebration was splendid, and no one regretted going to it. The food was excellent, the wine strong, and the guests danced and sang well into the night, as if the married couple were not parting, but rejoicing over a reunion. When the last of the guests had gone, the man embraced his wife, thanked her for all she had done for him, and said: "I shall never forget you, and I should like to give you something to remember me by. I beg you, take the most precious thing you can find in my house." The woman promised to choose something, and the man went to sleep.

As soon as her husband's eyes had closed, the woman called her servants. After first pinching her husband's hand to make sure he was asleep, she had him carried in his bed to her father's house. Then she sat on a wagon containing all her goods, and also returned to her father's house.

The man had drunk a good deal of wine at the feast, and it was almost noon when he woke up. He looked around him in wonder, and, not recognizing anything, called out in confusion: "Where am I? Where has my house gone?"

The door opened and his wife came in. "Where else would you be," she asked, "but in my father's house? Did you not tell me to take the most precious thing I could find? And I know that, not only in your house, but in the whole world, I should not find a treasure greater than you. I love you, and with the grace of God we may still have children." The couple embraced, and quickly set out to see Rabbi Simeon.

"Well," he greeted them cheerily, "do you still want me to divorce you?"

"Nothing of the sort!" cried the man. "There will be no divorce. You foresaw well enough what my wife would do, Rabbi, and I shall never cease to be grateful for your advice. Only now, I beg you, give us your blessing, that we may have issue as soon as possible."

Simeon ben Yohai did as the man asked. He gave the couple his blessing, and before the year was out a son was born to them. The man gave him the name Simeon. He would always remind the happy couple of Rabbi Simeon ben Yohai, their benefactor, whose wisdom and charity were never forgotten in the whole of Israel.

Joshua ben Levi
and the Angel of Death

At the time when the Jews were ruled over by the Romans, there lived in Lydda in the Holy Land a rabbi called Joshua ben Levi, who was wise, pious, and absolutely just. He never sinned against either God or man, and he kept his soul as clean as when the Creator had breathed it into him before sending him into the world. All the denizens of heaven rejoiced at the rabbi's deeds.

But every man is mortal, and however good he may be nothing can change that. After many years Joshua's days had run their course, and God called the Angel of Death to Him. "Find Rabbi Joshua ben Levi," he told the angel, "and carry his soul off to Paradise. But do not forget one thing: Joshua has been so just that you should fulfil his every wish first."

The Angel of Death promised to do all God asked of him, and flew down to earth. His face shone with many eyes, and in his right hand he held a drawn sword, with a drop of bile at its tip. All those on earth were terrified at the sight of him. Whenever people caught sight of the Angel of Death, their mouths would fall open in horror, and the angel would allow the bile to drop into them. Thus men died, and the Angel of Death sped on to his other victims whose fate was sealed.

When the Angel of Death appeared before Joshua ben Levi, the rabbi turned away in horror. "God wishes me to die?" he asked quietly.

"Such is His will," replied the angel, "and I have come to execute it. But you have a pure soul, so God has commanded me to grant you any wish you have before you die."

"In that case," said Joshua, "show me my place in Paradise."

The Angel of Death took a step towards the rabbi, in order to lead him to Paradise, but Joshua ben Levi jumped backwards in fright. "How am I to go with you," he sighed, "when I am afraid of your sword? Let me hold it, please, or I shall not dare to go with you."

So the angel gave the rabbi his sword of death and lifted him in his arms, and before Joshua ben Levi knew it he was standing before the walls of Paradise. The angel lifted him so high that Joshua could see the whole of Paradise spread out before him.

There were two diamond-studded gates leading into Paradise, each of them guarded by 70,000 seraphim. The glare of the diamonds was brighter than that of the sun, and their sparkle was reflected in the water of four great rivers, which fed the roots of the

9,000 trees of Paradise. Even the smallest of those trees gave off a perfume more delicious than the headiest of earthly blossoms. In the four corners of Paradise a choir of 7,000 cherubim sang songs of praise and thanksgiving. And in the very center of Paradise there stood two trees — the Tree of Knowledge, and the Tree of Life, whose leaves covered the whole of Paradise. This was a tree which gave off 500,000 different fragrances which seeped into every corner of Paradise, with its seven great houses, each containing thousands of chambers. One of these was reserved for Rabbi Joshua ben Levi.

When the just rabbi saw all this splendor, he had no desire to return to Earth. He delighted in the exquisite colors, was intoxicated by the angels' song, adored all the perfumes, and could not see enough of all the beauty. The arms of the Angel of Death, who was holding Joshua ben Levi up all the time, were beginning to ache. He shook the rabbi impatiently, and, at that, Joshua ben Levi took a firm grip on the edge of the walls of Paradise, jerked himself free of the Angel of Death, and with the sword of death in his hand, leapt into Paradise.

The Angel of Death was very angry. He shouted at Joshua, threatened him, and beseeched him to return the sword, but in vain. Joshua ben Levi walked around Paradise entranced, taking not the slightest notice of the angel. There was nothing the angel could do except to go shamefaced before God and complain about the impudent rabbi. But God loved Joshua dearly because of his pure soul, and it was seven years before He heard the angel's plea. It was only then that he ordered the rabbi to go back to Earth and return the angel's sword, and from that day on death returned to the earth.

The first to die was the rabbi himself. But because he had not forgotten the fear the Angel of Death had inspired in him, he got the angel to promise one more thing before his death: to swear not to show either his face or his sword to the dying. The angel kept his word. After that he stood before men invisibly, and only the godless, whose hearts were filled with fear, have since then thought on their deathbed that they saw the Angel of Death. The deadly envoy takes the souls of such as those the way one takes thorns from a skein of wool. But from the pious and the just, such as was Rabbi Joshua ben Levi, the Angel of Death takes the soul carefully and gently, as one would take a piece of thread from a bowl of milk; and he sends their souls straight to Paradise.

✡

Choni
Hame'agel

Long ago there lived in the Holy Land a pious man, the sage Choni. The people honored him as a saint. God looked upon him with favor and never refused him anything.

One year the land was afflicted by a great drought. The skies closed up, and there was not a drop of rain to moisten the parched earth. "What will become of us?" the Jews wailed. "If it goes on like this the grain harvest will fail, and we'll all starve to death." In their anxiety and fear they went to see Choni. "Choni!" they cried. "Only you can save us. Ask God to give us rain."

Choni agreed, and went out into the street. With his staff he drew a circle in the dust, stepped into it, and called out, "Lord, I shall not leave this circle until it is washed away by rain. Give us water, I beseech you, and do not leave your people without help!"

As soon as Choni had finished speaking, the sky darkened with rain clouds. They blotted out the scorching sun, and with them came a strong wind. Before anyone knew what was happening, a heavy downpour began. Choni watched as the torrential rain blotted out the circle he had drawn on the ground, and when it was quite gone he happily returned home. From that day forward Choni was known as Me'agel, or Drawer of Circles, and his fame grew greater than ever.

After the rain the countryside came to life again. Fields and gardens became green, the air was filled with fragrances, and even people seemed to burst into bloom: after a long absence their laughter returned, and their songs could be heard throughout the land. One morning Choni rode on his donkey to look at the countryside. On and on he went until, far beyond the town, he spied an old farmer planting a tree.

"Peace be with you, old man," Choni greeted him. "What is that tree you are planting?"

"It is a carob tree," replied the old man.

"And how long will it be before it bears fruit?"

"Seventy years."

Choni became thoughtful. "I respect your work," he said after a while, "but still I do not understand you. We do not even know what today will bring, yet you are making provision for the future. Why do you bother?"

"I am not a learned man like yourself," the old man told him, "so I shall answer you simply. I do only what I enjoy doing, and what my fathers did before me. The trees they planted still give me fruit, therefore I, too, plant trees, which will one day bear fruit for my grandchildren."

"Only God knows if you are right," Choni replied. "But one thing is certain: you have done enough work in your lifetime. You have not many years to run, and you would do better to rest."

With these words Choni took his leave of the old farmer and went his way. It was noon. Choni felt very hungry, so he rode his donkey towards a nearby cave, whose shade was most inviting. He tied the donkey up outside, sat down inside the cave and took out the bundle containing his bread. But just then the sage's body was overcome with such tiredness as he had never known before. His limbs grew heavy as though pressed to the ground by huge stones, and his eyelids began to droop. Before Choni had time to think, he had fallen to sleep. He slept on and on, and had no idea that the mouth of the cave had become overgrown with ivy. Its shoots grew faster and faster, and reached out towards Choni, until he, too, was covered with a network of branches, wound round him from head to foot. The whole place was steeped in silence. A strange magic divided the cave from the rest of the world. The spirit of sleep which reigned over it was not disturbed even by the song of a bird or the sigh of a breeze.

The years went by, and no one knew what had become of Choni. His son grew up and got married, his wife died, and those who knew him began to forget what he had looked like or what his voice sounded like. And days more passed, which ran into weeks, and the weeks into months and years; people went on being born and dying, but Choni did not return, and his name was remembered only by rabbis well versed in the holy books.

At long last the ivy which had wound its way around Choni dried out. The network which covered the sage's body fell apart, and he woke up. He left the cave, intending to hurry home, but all that was left of the donkey was a pile of bones. "Whatever has happened?" Choni asked in perplexity. He looked around him, and recognized nothing. There was a forest where there had once been fields — a garden where vines should have stood. There was no sign of people, except for a man not far away from Choni who was picking the fruit of a large tree. Choni went closer, and saw that the man's basket was full of locust-beans, the fruit of the carob tree.

"Peace be with you," Choni greeted the farmer. "I see you are gathering the fruits of your work."

The man looked at Choni in surprise. "You look intelligent enough," he said. "But you speak like a fool. Don't you know that it takes a carob tree seventy years to bear fruit? My grandfather planted this tree. He is long since dead, but as you see, his work was not in vain."

Choni's heart felt an icy chill. "Can I have slept for seventy years?" he thought, horrified. "Whatever will happen to me? Whom can I turn to?"

He went into the town where he had once lived, but he could find neither his house nor the street it had stood in. "Do you know the son of Choni?" he asked the passers-by, but one after the other shook his head. It was a long time before Choni met an old woman

who was able to answer him. "Choni's son is dead," she told him. "His property belongs to his son — you had better go and see him."

Choni asked the way to the house, and was soon standing in front of a building he could scarcely recognize as the family home. A tall man came out to meet him. "What do you want?" he asked.

"I am your father's father," Choni replied. "For seventy years I have been enchanted in a cave; but now the spell has passed, and I am returning home."

The man looked Choni up and down suspiciously. "If you want a piece of bread, why do you not say so?" he replied, sharply. "There is no need to invent crazy stories. Wait here, and I will bring you some food."

Choni blushed with shame, and his eyes filled with tears. Without a word he turned and walked away aimlessly. "My grandson does not know me," he said to himself bitterly, "but the learned men have surely not forgotten me." Choni looked around him and saw that he was standing in front of a synagogue. Stepping inside, he saw a group of rabbis studying the Torah. "O you who are erudite in the law of Israel," Choni addressed them, "allow me to learn with you the secrets of the Lord's teaching."

The rabbis took Choni into their group, and they studied together. Choni surpassed them all in learning, and there was no one as wise as he. "You are as wise," the oldest of the rabbis told him, "as Choni Hame'agel was in his time."

"But I am Choni!" the sage cried joyfully. "Do you not recognize me?"

But the rabbis turned away from him. "What lie is this?" they asked sadly. "Are you not satisfied with wisdom, that you would be honored as a saint?"

Choni left the synagogue even more crestfallen than he had entered it. He wandered the streets, asking after his friends and acquaintances, but they were all long dead. People passed by him without noticing he was there; not one of them so much as greeted him, no one invited him to his table. Choni was utterly alone, more solitary than a stranger in a far-off land.

"I know no one, and no one knows me," he whispered, bitterly. "What use is my knowledge to me? How much more fortunate was the man who planted the carob tree for his grandchildren. He lives in their memory — they remember him with love. But I am quite unnecessary. My grandson does not know me, and the learned men think I am a liar. Why am I still to live, Lord?"

He suddenly felt so tired that he longed to lie down. Leaving the town behind him, he walked without rest until he reached the familiar cliff. There he entered the cave, slumped exhausted to the ground, and died. Thus it was that God fulfilled his final wish. The ivy which covered Choni's body never disappeared from the cave again.

The Fox
and the Fish

A fox was walking along the bank of a river one day. He looked down into the water, and saw fish swimming anxiously to and fro. "Why don't you stay in one place?" asked the fox. "What are you afraid of?"

"Can't you see?" the fish replied. "There are nets spread out all around us. If we were not careful to avoid them, it would be the end of us."

The fox was hungry, so he said cunningly, "Poor things, you know nothing but fear and danger. You had better come out on dry land, where there are no nets. We shall live together as our forefathers did."

But the fish knew the fox's guile, and were not going to be caught like that. "You fool," they replied. "Do you really suppose we are so stupid? If we are in danger in the water, which is our element, how should we be threatened on dry land, which is not our home at all?"

Seeing that he was not going to outwit the fish, the fox went away disappointed.

The Fox
and the Vineyard

A hungry fox stood in front of a large vineyard. The very thought of the sweet grapes made his mouth water, but the vineyard was surrounded by a high wall, and try as he might the fox could not climb over it. He ran round the vineyard helplessly, until he noticed a small gap in the wall. He tried to get through it, but the hole was too small. "Why should I be in such a hurry to eat?" the fox asked himself. "I shall wait a while: when I am a little thinner, I shall be able to squeeze through into the vineyard and eat my fill." For three whole days the fox neither ate nor drank. His flanks grew slimmer, and he was able to slip through the hole in the wall without difficulty. The moment he got inside he began to pick the grapes. He gulped down one after the other, and did not stop until his belly was fit to burst. Then he tried to leave the vineyard. But the fox had forgotten one thing: while the hole in the wall had stayed the same, he had got fatter, so he got stuck in the wall and could not get out of the vineyard! What did he do? For three days he stayed stuck in the wall and ate nothing at all; when he had grown thin again he was able to leave the vineyard without trouble. "Vineyard, O vineyard," said the fox, ruefully, "how beautiful you are to look at, and how sweet your fruit is. But you are quite useless. I was hungry when I came to you, and I am hungry as I go away."

THE FIFTH
LIGHT

The Sephardic Jews
Living in the Orient
and in Southern
Europe

The Clever Son

Many years ago there lived in Jerusalem a rich Jewish merchant. He traveled widely, and saw many foreign lands, but most of all he liked to travel to Babylonia. That was where he did his best business, and what was more, his friend Ramai lived there.

One year the merchant decided to make a particularly big profit. He exchanged almost all his belongings for gold, and set off to visit Ramai, hoping to get really rich in his friend's land. But the journey was a bad one; the merchant fell ill, and that was the end of his trading. He lay in Ramai's house, and one doctor after another came to his bedside, but he had a feeling that there was no remedy for his sickness. So he called Ramai to him and said: "Soon I shall die, and leave here all the gold I brought with me. I have an only son, who is scarcely twenty years old. Be so kind as to hand over to him my gold, but only on condition that he can prove his cleverness three times. If he cannot, then give him enough not to go hungry, and keep the rest for yourself. It would be better for it to remain in your hands than for him to squander it." Ramai promised to do as he was asked, and soon after that the merchant died.

As soon as the funeral was over, Ramai sent the merchant's son a letter. "Your father died in my house," he wrote, "leaving here all his gold. I live in the greatest city in Babylonia, and my name is Ramai." Ramai deliberately omitted to write his address, and he asked all the inhabitants of the city not to tell any stranger where he lived. "I wish to test the cleverness of a certain young man," he added by way of explanation. Ramai's fellow citizens did not wonder at his strange request, and promised to help him.

It was not long before the son of the Jewish merchant arrived in Ramai's city. He asked the whereabouts of Ramai's house, but no one would tell him. "No matter," he said to himself, "I shall find out." He went up to an Arab who was selling wood in the market-place, and said, "Take two bales of firewood to the house of Ramai. Here is payment for your service."

The Arab lifted the wood onto his shoulder, and the son set off after him. When they arrived at Ramai's house, the master came out into the courtyard. "Why are you bringing me wood?" he asked the Arab. "I have not bought any."

"I am the one you should ask," said the merchant's son. "I have come from Jerusalem for my father's gold. No one would tell me where you lived, so I thought up this little trick."

"You are not stupid," Ramai replied. "Your father would be proud of you. So come in, and take a seat at my table. Such a rare guest as yourself deserves a fine luncheon."

Seven people sat down at table: the merchant's son, Ramai, his wife, his two sons and his two daughters. But there were only five roast chickens on the table. "Let us see whether our guest from Jerusalem will be as ingenious a second time," the master of the house said to himself. And he turned to the young man and said: "Divide up the chickens, please. But be sure to do it fairly!"

"I will do as you ask," the merchant's son replied, and he got to work at once. He placed the first chicken in front of Ramai and his wife, gave the second to his sons, the third to his daughters, and kept the remaining two for himself.

"Is that the custom in Jerusalem?" his host asked in surprise.

"That," replied the merchant's son, "is the language of numbers. I gave one chicken to you and your wife. That makes three altogether. Your two sons received one chicken, and your two daughters also. Both add up to three. So, since I am alone, I have taken two chickens, and that also makes three."

"A cunning lad," thought Ramai to himself. "Twice already he has shown his cleverness." But he kept his thoughts to himself, and after lunch took the young man into the city. While they were out walking, Ramai's wife cooked a hen. In the evening she put it on the table, and Ramai said to his guest: "We are the same number as at luncheon, but now there is only one hen. I wonder how you will divide it up this time?"

The merchant's son did not hesitate for a moment. Cutting off the bird's head, he gave it to his host, saying: "You are the head of the family, so this portion is yours. Since a mother and father are joined together like neck and head, the mistress of the house shall have the hen's neck. The two sons are the pillars of the family, on whose work its fortune depends. They should therefore have the hen's legs. The daughters will soon marry and leave the house — so what could be more fitting for them than the wings? That leaves the body of the bird, which I shall eat myself, since it is like the hull of the ship on which I left Israel, and on which I shall also return home."

When he had heard these words, Ramai brought the merchant's gold and said, "Your father asked that I should not give you your inheritance before you had thrice proven your cleverness. Without even knowing it, you have fulfilled the condition. Take, then, what is yours, and whenever you come to Babylonia again, you will be welcome in my house."

The merchant's son thanked Ramai for all he had done for his father and himself, rewarded him generously, and the next day sailed joyfully homeward to the Holy Land.

A Jew
in Athens

A certain young Jew from Jerusalem, well versed in the Torah and the laws of Israel, took the advice of his teachers and went out into the world to see new lands and different customs. The young man wandered from one country to another. He saw and heard many things, but even when he was far from his native country he did not forget that he was a Jew. He lived like his forefathers, and observed the customs they had passed down in everything he did. After some months the lad reached the famous city of Athens, in Greece.

One evening he went into an inn. The innkeeper placed some eggs on the table, and the young man paid for his supper and his bed for the night, and began to eat. When he had eaten his fill, he gave thanks to God for the food, and the innkeeper saw that he was a Jew. Since he disliked Jews, he decided to try to annoy his guest, and he brought two pieces of cheese from the kitchen.

"I see that you are from the Holy Land," the innkeeper said, mockingly, "so you are surely not short of wisdom. Be so kind as to tell me which cheese is from the milk of a black sheep, and which is from that of a white."

"My dear fellow," replied the young man, "you are older than I, and certainly your learning is greater. First tell me which of the eggs I have just eaten was laid by a white hen, which by a black, and then I will answer your question."

The innkeeper scowled. He had been looking forward to making fun of the young man from Jerusalem, but instead he had been put to shame himself. He soon thought of another malicious scheme, though. "A good thing I remembered!" he cried suddenly. "I almost broke the new law!"

"What new law is that?" the young man asked.

"It has been in force since yesterday," the innkeeper explained, "and it concerns you. Only those foreigners may sleep in Athens who can cross the street in three leaps. You have already paid for your bed, so while you are leaping across the street, I'll get your room ready."

The young man realized at once that the innkeeper was trying to get rid of him, so he said, "If you have such a law in Greece, then I should be glad to obey it. But I have never heard of it before, and I want to be sure to do it right. First you must show me how to jump across the street."

The innkeeper, delighted at having fooled the Jew so easily, left the inn and leapt across the street in three great jumps. But the young Jew lost no time in slamming the door shut and shooting both the bolts.

"What is the meaning of this?" cried the innkeeper. "Would you throw me out of my own house?"

"You have no reason to complain," replied the young man calmly. "I have only done to you what you would have done to me. You are the victim of your own customs, and now you will surely better understand the law which we Jews have: do unto others as you would have them do unto you."

So the man from Jerusalem slept well in the inn, and the next morning left Athens in a merry mood.

The Light
from the Fig Spring

How many nations there are on this earth! Some of them boast mighty armies, others the skills of their craftsmen. There are nations of fine sculptors and lands where the artists paint wonderful pictures. But God gave the Jews a special gift: he presented them with the Torah, the book of the Law, and ordered them to live by it. So from time immemorial they have carried the words of Holy Writ in their hearts, and they like nothing better than to read and study the Torah.

The people of Safed in the Holy Land were especially learned. The room set aside there for study was always full, whether it was the sun or the moon that lit up the sky. When a son was born, they could be sure he would study the Torah as zealously as his father before him, and when an old man died, they buried a sage. The Jews of Safed were the talk of the Land, and everybody considered it an honor to hear them speak.

Thus it was for many years. But one spring a new Arab ruler came to power in the city of Safed, and the Jews were the first to suffer at his hands. The ruler did not like the fact that the Jews were always studying the Torah, for he hated the Law. He was angry that they were teachers, and did not beg him for work in the fields. He would stop up his ears when he heard them chant sacred liturgies, and he hated to see the children hurrying with their fathers to the synagogue. One day he decreed: "If the Jews wish to marry, they shall pay for it." And as if that were not enough, the ruler soon demanded that they pay for funerals and for celebrating feast days; he increased taxes and introduced all manner of fines. What was allowed one day was forbidden the next, so that the Jews were deprived of practically all they earned. But they still managed to scrape together a living, and the ruler of the city noted with vexation that they were not nearly as downcast as he had hoped they would be.

"What can I do to make life even more difficult for the Jews?" he mused. "The more they pay me, the more pupils they have who gladly pay gold for a single word from the sages!"

"You must stop the Jews from studying all the time," said his counselor, who was as bad as the ruler himself. "But you must do it cleverly, so that they cannot complain to the sultan. Why don't you forbid them to burn lights at night? Issue a decree that they are not to light candles or oil lamps, and you will see that they will scarcely have enough to buy bread with!"

The ruler of the city did at once as his counselor advised him. When they heard the bad news, the Jews of Safed were very sad. They did not mind living an even more frugal existence than before, but they could not imagine spending the whole night in bed. "Can the Torah be taught only in the daytime?" they lamented. "Each minute without it seems an age! How are we going to live now?"

The parents' grief rubbed off on the children. Everyone spent the whole of that terrible day trying to think of a way to overcome this new obstacle, but neither young nor old came up with any ideas. Noon came and went, and the shadows began to lengthen; the Jews waited anxiously for night to fall on Safed.

Perhaps the saddest of all was little Chanan. "The old people are all right," he said to himself bitterly, "no one can take away from them what they have already learnt. But I shall never open a book at night. How can I ever learn what my teachers know?" Chanan wished he had the eyes of a cat, so he could see in the dark; then he longed for the wings of a bird, so he might fly far away, to a place where the Jews were not plagued by an unjust ruler. He began to daydream, and as he wandered through the animal world, an idea came to him. "What if I were to go to the Valley of the Mill?" he thought. "There are thousands of fireflies around the Fig Spring! They are like sparks of the forest, and when they are all joined together, they will shine like a flame."

Chanan set off at once. Darkness was falling, and the synagogue was as dark as an abandoned lighthouse. Chanan hurried through the narrow streets and soon left the city behind. It was a warm summer's evening; a stiff breeze was blowing off Mount Hermon. The sun had set, and the first star appeared in the sky. The path slowly began to descend. It twisted to the left and right, and the stars kept vanishing behind the tall trees. At last Chanan arrived at the Fig Spring. It rose in the middle of a deep valley, and everywhere he looked there was a tiny light floating in the air.

"Fireflies!" said Chanan, with a sigh of joy. Finding himself a big stick, he began catching the fireflies and sticking them to the end of it. Meanwhile, it had grown quite dark. Chanan ran hither and thither, adding one firefly after another to his stick, but time went by quickly, and the glow of the insects did not seem to get much brighter. The boy began catching them more wildly than ever; he had lost count of how many he had stuck to the end of his stick. He wound his way among the trees, tripping over their roots, but his efforts were to no avail. The stick he was holding in his right hand glowed only faintly, like the moon when it is hidden behind the clouds, and there was no question of reading by its light.

Chanan sat down on the ground. He was tired, and could scarcely catch his breath. He felt the dozens of small scratches which covered his arms and legs, but they did not burn nearly as fiercely as the thought that he would not be able to study the Torah as much as his father and his father's father had done. "I had hoped that the woodland sparks would light up the holy teaching for me," he sighed, "but they will not even give me enough light to see my way home."

As soon as he had said this, innumerable fireflies began to gather around Chanan. Thousands of tiny lights surrounded him, making a great glow in the middle of the night:

Chanan looked around him in amazement. Then he heard a faint little voice. "Chanan," it said in his ear, "I am the queen of the fireflies from the Fig Spring. My children fled you because they thought you were one of those wicked folk who catch them and kill them for pleasure. But if you wish us to light up the letters of the holy Torah, we should be glad to accompany you to Safed, for your God is our God, our Lord, our Creator."

Chanan set off home joyously. On the orders of their queen, all her firefly subjects from the whole of the Valley of the Mill set off after him, and he could not have seen his way more clearly even if he had had a bright torch. A swarm of fireflies flew along above him like so many little lamps. Soon Chanan reached the room which was set aside for study. There the learned men of Safed sat sadly in darkness and in silence. The moment Chanan entered, the room was filled with light. The sages cried out with joy. They praised Chanan and the fireflies, and sang and danced as if it were Simhat Torah, the feast of Rejoicing in the Law.

When the Arab ruler heard that the Jews had disobeyed his command, and that they had lit up the house of study, he was beside himself with anger. He took a company of soldiers and made his way to the house to punish them, but as he crossed the threshold he stopped. True, the Jews were studying the Torah, but not by the light of candles or oil lamps. The fireflies were circling around the students, illuminating the open pages of their books. The ruler was struck dumb with rage. He had said nothing of fireflies in his prohibition, so he could not punish the Jews. He didn't know which way to turn. His anger, shame and hatred welled up inside him until his heart broke. He fell dead to the ground, and from that time forth none of his successors has ever tried to stop the Jews of Safed from studying.

The Miraculous
Seed

In the land of a certain sultan lived a group of Jews whose ancestors had once lived in Jerusalem. The sultan and his subjects made it clear to the Jews that they were not welcome. They were given a few hovels on the edge of the capital city, and the only work they were allowed to do was mean and badly paid, so the Jews lived from hand to mouth.

There was one man who was especially poor. He carried water from morning till night, but for the pittance he earned doing that he could buy no more than a small piece of bread. He had a lot of children, and by the time he had divided it up among them there were only a few crumbs for each. The wretched father did not know what to do. He went out to work earlier and earlier, and returned home after dark, but all was in vain. Hunger had come to stay at his house, so in his desperation the man decided to try another way. He went to the market and mixed with the customers at the baker's stall. Then, when the baker was not looking, he stole a loaf of bread.

But those ill fortune has singled out do not escape it so easily. The baker noticed the theft right away, and the man was caught. The sultan's guard came, heard the witnesses, and before the poor fellow knew what was happening, led him off to the gallows. "Have you a last wish?" they asked him.

"What am I to wish?" replied the poor man, sadly. "In a while I shall be dead. It is only a pity that I shall take my secret with me to my grave. I am the only one who knows it; but if the sultan had any idea of what I know, he would surely give me a careful hearing."

The soldiers stopped their preparations. "Let us take him to the sultan," they said. "The gallows will wait, and perhaps he knows something which may prosper our realm."

When the sultan heard that the man who had stolen a loaf of bread at the market-place had a great secret, he gestured to all his courtiers to leave the chamber. "We are alone," he told the condemned man. "Speak!"

"Mighty sultan," the Jew began with a bow, "I know how to sow the seed of a pomegranate so that a tree grows up overnight. This secret was taught to me by my father, and it has been passed on from generation to generation in my family. If you wish, I can show you and your court my skill."

The sultan was overjoyed. He was not short of riches, but he loved the idea of being able to perform a miracle. So he gave orders for a pomegranate tree to be planted the next day. At the appointed hour the whole of the sultan's court gathered in the gardens. The man dug a small hole, took the seed of a pomegranate in his hand, and said to the sultan: "This seed will grow into a tree by tomorrow. But it must be planted by a man who has never stolen. Since I am a thief, I cannot plant the seed myself. If you will, O sultan, appoint someone in my place, and tomorrow you will be able to enjoy fresh pomegranates."

The sultan turned to his chief counselor. "Plant the seed," he ordered him, "and come here early tomorrow morning with the rest of the court. We shall all see whether a pomegranate tree really grows. Until that time the Jew is to be left alive!"

The next morning at dawn the sultan went out into the garden. He had not slept a wink all night, so great was his anticipation, but when he reached the place where his counselor had sown the seed, he grew very angry. All that he and his courtiers could see in the garden was the hole which had been dug in the ground, and there was not a sign of the rare tree.

The sultan had the condemned Jew brought to him. "You shall pay dearly for this!" he thundered. "Perhaps you thought you would escape in the night, but now you shall die such a death that you will regret your foolishness!"

The condemned man looked at the sultan steadily. "I had no wish to escape," he said, "and I stand by what I promised. The only reason the pomegranate did not grow is because your counselor did not fulfil the condition. He must have stolen something, which is why the tree did not come up."

"What have you to say to that?" the sultan asked his counselor.

The counselor blushed with shame. "Your excellency," he stammered in confusion, "the Jew is right. Many years ago I took a ring which dropped from your table and rolled under the carpet. Have mercy on me, I beg of you. I will return at once what does not belong to me."

The sultan frowned, and asked his treasurer to plant the seed. But after what he had seen, not even the treasurer was willing to try his hand. He shuffled his feet nervously, and after a moment said quietly: "O sultan, you know what a lot of riches I handle every day. I record each piece of gold and each diamond in the book, but once I could not resist, and took a rare pearl, which I did not enter in the book. I swear I will bring back the pearl this very day, and beg you not to be angry with me for my theft. But now I have told you the truth, you surely realize that I cannot plant the tree."

The sultan surveyed his subjects angrily, trying to choose one of them; but the condemned Jew spoke first: "Mighty sultan, it would be better not to ask any of them to plant the tree. A man can trust only himself; it will therefore be wisest for you to plant the seed."

There was a deep silence. Neither courtiers nor sultan spoke. Finally the sultan said: "I confess that even I am not blameless. When I was a small boy, I took a precious inlaid needle from my mother."

"There you are, sultan," said the Jew. "None is mightier than you, and each of your courtiers has all he needs; yet neither you nor any of them can say he has never stolen. But I, who have not enough to keep my children from starving, am to die because I stole a piece of bread."

The sultan smiled. "I see," he said, "that your greatest secret is cleverness; but you cannot pass that on to anyone. For your boldness and wit, I pardon you your theft. I shall pay the baker, and you may go in peace."

The sultan ordered that the Jew be given generous gifts, and he and his family never went hungry again.

The Best Physician

Long after the Jews had been exiled from their own land and dispersed throughout the world, there lived in the Spanish city of Cordoba a well-respected and educated Jew called Maimon. Though he was nearly thirty, he had not yet found himself a wife. He lived alone, and would probably never have married at all, had he not had a strange dream one night. An old man with a long beard appeared to him and said, "Go into the neighboring city, and marry the daughter of a butcher. A son will be born to you who will be the pride of Israel one day." At first Maimon took no notice, but after the vision had come to him several more times he did as the old man had instructed him. He went to the neighboring city, found a butcher, and asked him for his daughter's hand in marriage.

Less than a year after the bride and groom had drunk together from their nuptial cup their son Moses came into the world. When Moses ben Maimon grew up, there was not another Jew who could match his wisdom. He wrote learned books, and for many years was a teacher to the children of Israel. Maimon earned great renown not only as a sage, but also as a physician. He cured many a monarch, and they did not forget their deliverer. Maimon would help the Jews whenever they were in need. He shielded his brothers from slander and warded off every peril by his intercession. The Jews were grateful to him, but their enemies detested him.

One day word of Maimon's healing art reached the ears of the mighty sultan of Egypt. His own physician had just died, so the sultan offered Maimon the office. Maimon accepted, but had he wrapped venomous snakes around his body, he could have done no worse for himself. A dozen of the best physicians in Egypt had vied for the privilege of treating the sultan, and now a foreigner, and even worse, a Jew, had got the job. All the physicians in the sultan's realm envied Maimon, and lost no chance to slander him to their ruler.

Shortly after Maimon arrived at court, a learned dispute arose between him and his rivals. "Such is our skill," the Egyptian doctors claimed, "that we are able to return sight to those who are blind from birth."

"That is impossible," Maimon objected. "Only he who has once been sighted can be cured of blindness."

The Egyptian physicians went at once to the sultan and told him of the dispute. "We shall prove to you that we are right," they assured their ruler. "Then at least you will see that Maimon has no notion of true medicine."

The next day a blind man was brought before the sultan. "This poor fellow has been blind from birth," the Egyptian doctors claimed. Then one of them rubbed the patient's eyes with a fragrant ointment, and the man started to laugh and dance. "I can see!" he cried joyously. "For the first time I can see!"

The sultan turned to Maimon, and was about to cast doubt on his skills, when the court physician strode over to the newly-cured patient. Unfolding a handkerchief in front of the man's eyes, he asked: "What have I in my hands?"

"A red handkerchief," the man replied.

Maimon laughed and turned to the sultan. "O mighty lord," he said, "since when can those who see for the first time recognize colors?"

The sultan saw that the whole incident had been staged to discredit Maimon, and angrily drove the rival physicians from his palace. After that the Egyptian physicians hated the Jew more than ever. Maimon was aware of their spite with every step he took, and it was not long before his rivals tried again. They slandered him at every opportunity, and in the end even the sultan's counselors began to say: "You should take a second physician who is of our blood. You are too trusting, and might one day regret it." And they suggested at once that the sultan might be treated by one Kamun as well as by Maimon.

"What do I need two physicians for?" the sultan asked. "One is enough. But if you think that Kamun is as skilled as Maimon, I shall put them both to the test. We shall see which of them is the better physician, and that is the one I shall keep."

The sultan summoned Maimon and Kamun, and said, "Both of you are masters of your craft; but only one of you will be entrusted with caring for my health. Each of you must try to poison the other. Whichever of you stays alive will be proven superior, and he shall be my physician."

Kamun went away in a merry mood. His poisons had already disposed of several people, and he was quite sure he could get rid of Maimon. Maimon, on the other hand, was very sad. He had no wish to die, but neither did he want to kill anyone. He pondered day and night how he might solve the problem, but after much consideration he was no nearer to a solution than before. Several days passed. All the time Kamun was waiting impatiently for his chance. When he finally managed to mix a deadly poison in with Maimon's food, he was sure that the sultan's test had been decided in his favor. But Maimon knew what to do. He prepared an antidote, and the next day appeared before the sultan alive and well, as if nothing had happened. Kamun scowled with disappointment, and anxiously awaited a second chance to catch Maimon off guard. But Maimon did not even think of poisoning his rival. He just went on with his work, taking care to protect himself from Kamun's intrigues. But whenever he saw Kamun he said, "Be careful; I have something for you."

It was not long before Kamun had another poison ready, and after that he tried one after another on Maimon, but none of them took effect. Kamun became uneasy. "Maimon

has escaped everything," he said to himself, "and who knows what he is giving me." Kamun boiled for himself all manner of potions to protect himself from being poisoned, and swallowed everything he could think of, until his insides burned like fire. But in front of the courtiers he boasted: "I got the better of Maimon again; he put the most terrible of poisons in my wine, but he won't catch me out."

But it was more difficult for Kamun to deceive himself. Try as he might, he was unable to discover a single attempt by Maimon to poison him, and he began to think that his rival had prepared a particularly devilish substance which took effect very gradually. As soon as Kamun began to consider this possibility, he stopped taking any food, except for milk, which had to be from a cow that was milked before his eyes. It was not long before the Egyptian physician began to waste away. He grew pale; his cheeks became sunken and his hands began to shake. He could no longer even mix new poisons to try out on Maimon.

Early one morning Maimon was passing Kamun, who had just drunk his usual jug of milk. The Jew was a picture of health, and when Kamun saw how well his rival looked, he could have burst with rage. Suddenly Maimon stopped. Pointing to the jug of milk in Kamun's hand, he said, "Look what you are drinking!"

The moment Kamun heard those words, his heart began to pound. "I have drunk poison!" he thought, horrified. "I am poisoned!" And he put down the half-empty jug, and shakily set off to find a cure. But he had scarcely taken three steps when he fell down dead.

The sultan came at once, accompanied by his counselors, astrologists and alchemists. They all wanted to know what poison had killed Kamun, but Maimon refused to answer their questions. Then he had a small boy brought, and gave him the milk which was left in Kamun's jug. The child drank it without coming to any harm. At that moment the sultan's counselors began to shout: "The Jew kills by magic! Put him to death!"

But Maimon answered calmly, "What magic do you speak of? Kamun died of fear and a bad conscience." Then he told the story to all who were present, and when he had finished there was no one who did not believe him. The sultan rejoiced at his physician's wisdom. He gave Maimon a royal reward and said to him: "Now I know which is the best physician of all. Those who can cure the body are legion, but your art is also with the soul. Stay, then, in my service, and I promise that both you and your people shall prosper in my land."

Maimon agreed to the sultan's request. He cared for the sultan's health, and there was never another contender for his office in the whole of Egypt.

More Than
Just a Dream

In the famous Arab city of Cairo there were once many synagogues. Some were large and some were small; some had marble pillars, others wooden floors, but one thing they had in common. When the hour of prayer came, they were packed so tight with Jews that people could hardly bow to their God without bumping into each other.

One of the most pious of men was Isaac Luria. He never missed a prayer session, so even if the synagogue was full no one would occupy his seat in the pew. But one day a stranger sat in Luria's place. When Luria arrived he sat down beside him somewhat ungraciously, and opened his prayer-book. Then he began to feel a strange curiosity. He leaned over towards the stranger, and what should he see! The book the other man was holding was full of deep mysteries.

Luria forgot the rest of the world. He became engrossed in the strange symbols; word by word and sentence by sentence he fathomed the secret instructions, and he did not even notice that the service was long since over. All the rest of the congregation had departed, and where the stranger had been sitting there lay the open book.

From that day forth Luria changed completely. He left the city and went to live in a small cottage on the banks of the Nile, where he studied the mysterious book day and night. No one knew it had been sent to him by God, or that Luria's spirit rose up to heaven every night. There it would learn from all the sages who were long dead, and in the morning, when the saint's body was reunited with his soul, Luria would reveal great secrets. Soon Jews came to visit him from far and wide and Luria would read their faces like scrolls of parchment; he knew what they had done in their lives, and what awaited them in the future. He could see right away if a man was good or evil.

Once, shortly before the beginning of the Sabbath, the day of rest, Luria saw four travelers approaching his house. They walked slowly, as though they had come a long way, and their faces were troubled. Luria went outside. He was dressed in the white robe which he put on to welcome the Sabbath, and he seemed to shine like an angel which has just landed on earth. When the travelers saw him, they halted, filled with awe. But Luria smiled at the newcomers kindly, and asked: "What has brought you here? Tell me of your troubles before the holy Sabbath begins, that you may spend it in joy and peace."

"How can we rejoice?" the men replied, in subdued voices. "Our hearts are full of grief, and the Sabbath only brings our doom a day nearer."

"Speak!" Luria told them.

Then the three men told him how the king of their distant land had conceived in his heart a hatred for the Jews, and had ordered that within three months they should pay an enormous sum of money into his coffers. "If they do not pay the money," the king had decreed, "one half of the Jews will be slain, and the other half sold into slavery." The king's messengers had set out at once and spread his command throughout the kingdom. But the sum demanded was too high, and the Jews had less than half the amount the king had stipulated. "We could not pay such a ransom even if all the tears we have shed were of pure gold," the men told Luria. "But we had heard of you, of your great power and the miracles you perform with a mere word. Help us, we beseech you; avert the great peril which threatens us!"

"Do not be afraid," Luria said, "and do not despair. Sadness does not befit the Sabbath. Stay here until the holiday is over, and tomorrow you will see that your journey has not been in vain."

The next day, as soon as the Sabbath was over, Luria told the four travelers to take a strong rope and follow him to a nearby field. He stopped beside a deep well. "Throw one end of the rope into the well," he instructed them, "and when I give the word, haul it back up again."

The four did as they were bidden. They thought their task would be easy, but to their surprise they had a difficult time of pulling the rope back up. It tugged against them as though there were some heavy object on the end of it, and by the time they had done as Luria asked they were at the end of their strength. At last the end of the rope appeared over the rim of the well, and it was only then that they saw why they had been obliged to pull so hard. The rope was tied to the legs of a great golden bed, upon which a king in a silk nightgown lay fast asleep.

"It is he!" cried the travelers in astonishment. "Our ruler, who wishes to destroy us!"

Luria motioned to the men to be silent, and began to shake the king. The monarch woke up, and looked around in bewilderment. But Luria did not give him much time to think. He thrust into the king's hands a bucket without a bottom, and said, "I have heard that you require of my brothers something they are not able to give you. Then you shall empty the well of water before daybreak!"

"How can I do that?" cried the king, wretchedly. "The bucket has no bottom!"

"And have the Jews in your land the wherewithal to pay you?" Luria replied. "You know well enough that even if they were to sell all that they own, they could not raise the required sum. Consider carefully: either you will be obliged to empty the well with this bottomless bucket, or you will at once sign and put the royal seal on a document to say that the Jews have paid in full."

"I'll sign," sobbed the king. "I'll do whatever you want, only let me return to my palace in peace!"

"First your signature!" Luria ordered. He took out a scroll on which it was written that the Jews no longer owed their monarch anything, and had the king sign and seal it.

"Now you are free," Luria told the king. "Would you prefer to walk home, or to use the well?"

"I should like to go back the same way I came," the monarch replied.

"Lie down, then," Luria ordered him. Then he motioned to his companions, and they let the king and his bed back down the well.

At dawn Luria took his leave of the travelers. He gave them the parchment which guaranteed the safety of the Jews in their country, and his guests set off home joyfully. But their king had a much more disagreeable awakening. When he opened his eyes he was covered in sweat, and he dared not even tell his dream-tellers what he had dreamt. "What a terrible apparition!" he said to himself. "How fortunate that I was only dreaming!"

The king was more angry than ever with the Jews on account of the unpleasant events of the night. He waited impatiently for the day the money was to fall due, passing the time by thinking up ever more cruel punishments for his Jewish subjects. When the hour came, envoys from the Jews appeared before the king.

"Where is the money?" roared the king. "Pay up at once!"

"We have already paid," the Jews replied calmly, holding up the scroll. "Surely you recognize your own signature and seal."

When the king saw the parchment bearing his own signature and the royal seal, he was scared out of his wits. He fell to the ground in a faint, and it took more than an hour for the royal physicians to revive him. Then he said to the Jews in a strained voice, "What you say is true. I warrant that your brothers' and sisters' lives will be safe."

The monarch decreed that no one must harm a hair of any Jew's head, and the Jews rejoiced at the miracle which had saved them.

A Father's
Advice

In a certain capital city renowned for its mosques and synagogues lived an old Jew who had an only son. He brought the boy up in piety, and since the young man was also good-looking and skilful, he became the chief servant at the sultan's palace. He laid the table, brought food for the sultan and his family, poured their wine, and supervised the preparation of their meals.

The young man soon won the sultan's favor, and the old man rejoiced to see what good fortune had come his son's way. But the joy of father and son was to be short-lived. The father fell ill, and he could see from the doctors' faces that he was not going to recover. So he called his son and said to him, "Soon I shall die, and you will be left alone in the world. I have no fear for you, but if you wish to live for a long time, do not forget two things: if you should pass the synagogue and hear people praying there, go inside and join them. And if you are in the house of prayer, wait there until the service is over." Then the old man embraced his son and died.

As a sign of mourning the young man tore his prayer shawl, or *tallith*, and when he had buried his father he did not leave the house for a full seven days, as the ancient law demanded. After that, he returned to the palace. But one glance at the sultan was enough to tell him that something was wrong. The sultan glared at his servant, and the lad tried in vain to discover why his master was angry with him. He did not know that in his absence the vizier had persuaded the sultan that the young man was planning to poison him. From then on the sultan could not stand him. He had the young man taste everything he was to eat and drink, and gave orders for him to be followed secretly wherever he went.

One day the sultan went out for a ride near his palace. He gave his horse the rein and let it go where it wanted, and eventually arrived at the place where his subjects were firing limestone. The sultan watched them for a while, until his hatred brought a sudden idea to his head. Beckoning the oldest of the lime-burners, he said, "Tomorrow morning I shall send you a messenger. I want you to throw him at once into the hot kiln."

The man promised to obey the order, and the sultan returned to the palace. That evening, when the young man brought his master's food, the sultan told him: "Early tomorrow morning you are to go to the lime-works, find the oldest of the workers there, and tell him 'The king orders you not to forget your promise'. You should set off early — I shall not be requiring you at breakfast time."

The young man bowed to his master, and went to bed, so as not to oversleep in the morning. But it was a long time before he fell asleep. His heart was heavy, and his mind was troubled with an unpleasant foreboding. But the vizier spent a merry night. The sultan had told him what he planned to do, and the vizier celebrated the young man's death in advance. He sent for large amounts of wine, and the women of the harem danced for him until daybreak.

As soon as the young man woke up, he saddled his horse and set off. He rode and rode, until suddenly he heard the chanting voice of the prayer-leader who was reading the morning prayers in a synagogue on the edge of the city. The young man pulled up his horse. "I shall take my father's advice," he said to himself. "First I shall pray with my brothers, then I shall hurry to deliver the sultan's message." He entered the synagogue, and stayed there until the men inside had said their last amen and begun to fold their talliths.

As the young man prayed, the vizier was still drunk from the last night's wine. He was impatient for the sultan's servant to die, and he decided to go and watch the murder. He had a horse saddled, and rode as quickly as he could to the lime-works. Thus it happened that he arrived there before the young man. He looked around him, and when he could not see the young man's horse anywhere, he called over the oldest of the lime-burners. "I hope you have not forgotten the sultan's orders," he said to him.

The moment the vizier had said this, the lime-burner grabbed him around the waist, and before the vizier knew what was happening he had disappeared into the roaring kiln. It was at that moment that the young man arrived on the scene. "What have you done?" he called to the lime-burner. "Why have you killed the vizier?"

"Don't worry," the lime-burner replied. "The sultan gave orders that I was to throw the messenger he sent me into the kiln. That is exactly what I have done."

When the young man heard this, he began to tremble with horror. "What a terrible fate the sultan had prepared for me," he thought to himself. "If I had not followed my father's advice and entered the synagogue, it would have been the end of me." Filled with anxiety, he returned to the palace and went before the sultan.

"Why have you not obeyed my command?" cried the sultan.

"I did as you asked," replied the servant, quietly. "But the vizier got there first, and the lime-burner threw him into the kiln."

At these words a deep silence fell. For a long while the sultan stared at the ground; then he said, "I was possessed by some evil spirit when I believed the vizier. He said you wanted to poison me. He wished you to die, and he has paid for his malice. Instead of having the pleasure of seeing you die, he was himself punished. I no longer doubt your loyalty, and I hope you will continue to serve me as faithfully as before."

Bashi
and the Devil

There lived in Smyrna a certain merchant called Bashi, who had a wicked wife. She was as proud as a princess and just as vain and overbearing. She wanted new clothes all the time, but she didn't know what work was, so she just kept telling Bashi: "Buy me a new bracelet! Bring me some silk from the market!" Poor Bashi didn't know whether he was coming or going, but try as he might he could not satisfy her. If he brought white silk, she would send him back for blue. If he brought blue, she would want yellow. Night after night Bashi had to put up with her complaints that he didn't look after her properly — and that was not all. His wife was bad-tempered as well, and she would start a quarrel with him whenever she could. If he said it was sunny outside, she would retort that it looked like rain, and send him out to take in the washing. If he said the holiday began on Tuesday, she would say it did not start till Wednesday. Then she would have nothing ready, but the blame would be on Bashi. Thus it went on from day to day. Bashi's wife yelled at him day and night until she set the cooking pots ringing. So one day Bashi decided to run away. He crept quietly out of the house, and then ran and ran, until he was sure his wife would not catch him.

Bashi wandered from place to place, and as he was walking along he met a man at a crossroads. He told the man his story, and the man embraced him. "Brother!" he cried, "you and I are in the same boat. Though I am a powerful devil and an evil spirit, I, too, must flee my wife. When she starts screaming she makes more noise than thousands of drums, pipes, cymbals and trumpets all at once. I am afraid of wild beasts; I tremble lest I be bitten by a snake or pecked to death by an eagle. But even if all that were to happen to me, I should be better off than if I had stayed at home."

The devil related to Bashi all the torments he had had to endure, and at the very thought of his wife he wept as if his trials were still continuing. "I am glad that I met you, Bashi," he said afterwards. "We both have hard times behind us, and if you wish we can soon forget our troubles."

"What am I to do?" asked Bashi.

"Join forces with me," the devil proposed. "Listen carefully. We'll proclaim that you can cure every disease. You will become famous, then I'll enter into the bodies of all the kings of the earth and possess them. I shall so exhaust their strength that they

will suppose their last hour has come. There is no remedy that will cure them. Then you offer your services. When you give the word I shall depart from the kings' bodies; then the relatives will offer you rich rewards, and we'll share the profits. We'll go from one kingdom to another, and before we have got half way round the world we'll be the richest fellows under the sun."

Bashi was delighted with the idea, so they continued their journey together. Soon they came to a large kingdom. The devil led Bashi through the streets, praising his skill as a physician, and when the news of the wonderful healer had reached the king himself, the devil entered his body. No one could cure the mysterious ailment. The king began to waste away; the royal physicians were powerless, and before long the queen herself came to Bashi to ask him to cure her husband.

"I will do as you ask," said Bashi, "if you give me ten thousand guilders."

"The entire royal treasury contains only twenty thousand guilders," replied the queen, "but if you can cure the king in three days, I will give you what you ask. There is only one condition: if you do not succeed, you shall be executed."

"Agreed," Bashi said, and he asked to be left alone with the patient. The king was asleep. "It is I," Bashi told the devil in the king's body. "We shall get ten thousand guilders from the queen. You can come out now."

The other laughed. "Why should I come out?" he asked mockingly. "I am an evil spirit, and I only joined up with you to see your death."

"What about our agreement?" gasped Bashi, desperately.

"What about it?" chuckled the devil, and would say no more no matter how much Bashi beseeched him.

Dejected, Bashi left the king's chamber, hoping the devil would relent the next day, but the latter took no notice of his pleas either the second day or the third. "I want to see you die," he repeated. "And I do not intend to forego that pleasure. So you can stop your beseeching — you are only wasting your time."

When Bashi saw that there was no changing the devil's mind, he asked for an audience with the queen. He fell on his knees before her, and with eyes full of tears, he said, "I know that I was to have cured the king by today, but give me another three days. If you put me to death, no one else will cure him, and he will be dead before I am buried."

The queen looked at Bashi sternly. After a moment's silence she said, "I shall wait another three days. But if you wish to deceive me, your hopes are in vain. You shall not escape death, and what is more your end will be far more unpleasant than it was to have been."

Overcoming his fear, Bashi said, "I shall pray to my God, and do all I can to bring back the king's health. But I need your help, also, O queen. Have the king taken into the greatest hall in the palace, and summon musicians from all over the realm. Have them bring their trumpets, pipes, drums and fiddles, and await my orders."

The queen did as Bashi had asked. The sun rose and set twice, and on the third and last day the royal palace was full of musicians. There were exactly 5,555 of them. "When I open the doors of the hall where the king is lying," Bashi told them, "make a great din. Bang your drums, blow your pipes and trumpets, stamp your feet, and do not stop until I nod my head."

Then Bashi went into the hall where the king lay. He opened the doors, and at that moment all 5,555 musicians began to play furiously. No one had ever heard such a din in his life. The glass in all the palace windows shattered; the palace itself shook from its foundations to its roof, and the banging and wailing could be heard a thousand miles away.

"What is going on?" the devil called from the king's body. "What's all that racket?"

Bashi stepped up to the ailing monarch. The king lay motionless, hardly breathing, and did not notice Bashi at all. "Devil in the king's body," he said. "You made a fool of me. Soon I shall die; but I am still more fortunate than you. Your wife heard you were here, and she has come to fetch you."

"Indeed!" cried the devil, "only my wife rages so!" And he did not waste a minute more, but rushed out of the king's body and ran as fast as his legs could carry him until he could hear the terrible music no more.

The king sat up on his bed, healthy and strong, as if he had just woken up from a long dream. The queen embraced her husband and, late that night, when the musicians stopped playing, she paid Bashi the money he had been promised. The very next morning the merchant sailed far away across the sea. Only then was he sure his wicked wife would never find him. He made his home among the Jews of another land, and knew neither want nor tribulation to the end of his days.

Two
Mountains

There once lived in the Yemen two boys called Beinush and Elkana. When they were small they toddled about the yard together. When they grew up a little they sat under a tree and learned Hebrew letters together in its shade. When they grew up even more, they were taught how to read correctly from the scroll of the holy Torah. From morning till evening they never left each other's side, and parted only when their mothers called them home.

Beinush and Elkana had no secrets from each other. They could even read each other's thoughts by the expressions on their faces. There was only one thing which troubled them both: neither Beinush nor Elkana could play a musical instrument, and when they sang it sounded worse than the bleating of sheep at pasture. If the two of them had not been born in the Yemen, it would not have mattered so much. But the Yemeni Jews were music-lovers, and those who knew how to play an instrument were respected almost like rabbis. Musicians had all doors open to them, and there were few skills so admired. They sang differently on workdays and on holidays, differently in summer and in winter. And when the Jews of the Yemen played their instruments, that was really something! When they plucked the strings, when they took up their pipes, cymbals and drums, even the choirs of angels in heaven were silent, not wanting to miss that exquisite music.

The older Beinush and Elkana got, the more their shortcoming troubled them. They had no appetite for food and drink, and whenever they heard someone singing or playing melodiously, tears would come to their eyes. The whole village knew that something was troubling the two boys, but only their old teacher Ahuvia knew what it was. One afternoon, as he was explaining to them a passage of Holy Writ, he paused and said: "I know what is troubling you, and I may be able to give you some good advice. Far away from here, beyond the great desert, deep ravines and wild torrents, is the wondrous Mountain of Song. Its name is Zamar, and it rises to heaven itself. From foothills to peak it is covered with stones in the shape of musical instruments: there are flutes, pipes, citharas, cymbals, drums. Whoever sits down on one of those stones learns at once to play the instrument, and the melodies which he then hears inside himself, he will be able to sing beautifully. But the mountain does not help everyone; its gifts are only for those whose parents are without sin and whose hearts are pure. He who does not have such parents, or who is sinful himself, will be punished by the mountain."

Beinush and Elkana scarcely heard the last sentence. The moment Ahuvia mentioned the wonderful stones, the boys blushed with excitement, and wanted to set out at once. But the Mountain of Song was too far away, and Beinush and Elkana had first to prepare for their journey. Ahuvia explained to them which way they must go; the boys took plenty of food with them, and the next day they took leave of their parents, and set off.

The boys wandered for many weeks and months. They safely crossed the endless desert, passed through the deep ravines, and finally swam across the raging rivers. The nearer they got to the Mountain of Song, the fewer people they met. There were fewer and fewer animals to be seen; then even the birds started to disappear, as if they knew that a mountain full of music had no need of their song.

One morning at dawn, as the boys emerged from the wood in which they had spent the night, they saw in front of them a huge mountain. It was covered from top to bottom with stone instruments. "Mount Zamar!" cried Beinush and Elkana. "The Mountain of Song! We are here!"

The boys quickly ran up the mountainside. Now they sat on cymbal-shaped stones, now on stone trumpets. Beinush waved at Elkana from a stone drum, and Elkana at Beinush from a boulder in the shape of a cithara. They spent several hours in this way. When the hour for afternoon prayer came, they went down to the foot of the mountain again. A wonderful melody filled Beinush's head. One note followed another, unwinding like a thread from an endless skein, and in a beautiful voice he sang a song the like of which had never been heard. He clapped in time with himself, and suddenly began to play on the pipe he had brought with him such a happy tune that he himself could not resist dancing.

But Elkana returned crestfallen, his head hung low. The boy's hands hung limply by his side, as though all life had gone out of them; his face was pale, and his lips quivered. Beinush, full of joy, embraced his friend, but then stepped back with a start. "What has happened to you, Elkana?" he asked. "Can't you hear the music? Don't you want to sing and play, as though your body had been made for nothing else?"

Elkana was silent, shaking his head weakly.

"Answer me at least!" cried Beinush, shaking his friend.

Then Elkana fixed him with his gaze, put his index finger to his lips in the manner of those who cannot speak, and made an incomprehensible sound.

Suddenly, Beinush remembered the warning of their teacher Ahuvia. "The mountain has punished you, Elkana," he gasped. "You are dumb. Let us go home quickly: perhaps the wise Ahuvia can help you."

Without delay the boys set off homeward, but their journey was not an easy one. How could Beinush rejoice, when his friend had encountered such misfortune? And Elkana could scarcely put one foot in front of the other, could hardly see his way for tears.

The moment Ahuvia saw the boys, he knew what had happened. "Did I not tell you," he said reproachfully to Elkana, "that the gifts of the mountain were only for those whose parents were without sin and who had a pure heart? Luckily, I know how to get your speech back for you. Tomorrow morning bring your mother, your father, and nine men. As soon as prayers are over we shall set out for Dibur, the Mountain of Speech."

Elkana did as Ahuvia had told him, and the next day the small party set out. After they had been walking for several hours, high cliffs appeared on the horizon in front of them. When the group reached them, Ahuvia found a narrow footpath, along which he led them higher and higher, then suddenly down again. Amidst the cliffs, hidden by the other peaks, stood Mount Dibur.

"This mountain, the Mountain of Speech, is linked with the Mountain of Song by a secret magic," Ahuvia told them. "If Elkana is guilty of some sin, let him confess it on the mountain in front of all of us. Dibur will allow him to speak, and he will cease to be dumb. But if Elkana has nothing to say, then one of his parents has sinned. If he or she admits what has so far been concealed, their son will be released from his curse."

The party climbed up the Mountain of Speech. Surrounded by the nine men, Ahuvia stood before Elkana and his parents and asked them to speak. Elkana shook his head, as did his mother. But after a moment's hesitation his father said: "I confess that years ago I wrongfully accused my neighbor. I was jealous because he had a better harvest than I, and I said he was a thief. I bribed the witnesses at the court and the innocent man had to pay a heavy fine."

The moment the man had finished speaking, his son's speech returned. But no one rejoiced; all looked darkly at Elkana's father, and he stood shamefacedly, not knowing where to turn his eyes.

"You shall return to your neighbor what is his," Ahuvia told the guilty one. "And let the punishment which was inflicted upon your son be sufficient warning for you next time." Ahuvia fell silent, then continued. "It is written that a dry bale will set fire to a wet one. Thus the sin of one man may afflict the innocent. We are all joined together;

therefore each of us answers for the others, and this is the only way for us to remain pure."

Beinush, who had learnt to play and sing on the Mountain of Song, was the first in the village to hear of the words of the wise Ahuvia. He then traveled throughout the Yemen, and there was no musician more renowned than he. He refreshed the weary, cheered the sad. People were happiest when Beinush sang them a song of two mountains, the Mountain of Song and the Mountain of Speech. So their secret was not forgotten, but no one has since been able to find the mountains.

The Ransom
of Abraham ibn Ezra

Many years ago there lived in Toledo a man called Abraham ibn Ezra. He knew many things, and his brow concealed wondrous thoughts. When he spoke of the holy Torah, God's teaching was opened up to those who had never learned it before. When he sat with his pupils beneath the night sky, he knew the stars so well, they might have had their names written on them. Abraham was able to read the books of other nations, and he translated them, but he also wrote down what he felt in his heart, and his poems, songs, tales and riddles were known to all the Jews of Toledo.

One thing troubled Abraham. He was never short of pupils, but what use to him was that, when he was poorer than a beggar? He could not buy bread with words: for that he needed money, and Abraham wanted nothing more than to be able to earn himself a few coppers.

The trouble was that Abraham ibn Ezra was the unluckiest fellow that ever there was. He inherited a little money from his father, and wished to go into business; but before he could buy any goods someone had stolen the money. He took up tax-collecting — and had to pay off the debt left by the previous tax-collector. He became the servant of a synagogue — in a few days he was wandering the streets again, for the wind had torn the roof off the synagogue. Whatever Abraham turned his hand to was blighted with misfortune, and his only consolation was his poems.

"What am I to do," he said to himself one day, "so as not to have to live on alms? If I were to start selling shrouds, then people would surely stop dying. If I were to sell candles, then the sun would no longer set, and there would be daylight all night long. The best thing I can do is to leave Toledo. Perhaps I shall be more fortunate somewhere else."

So Abraham began to live even more modestly than before, and saved up enough from the gifts he received so he could leave Toledo. One morning he boarded a ship which was bound for distant shores. He stood watching the shoreline till it disappeared from view, and turned over in his mind the fate which awaited him on the other side. But fortune had decreed that his journey would end quite differently.

Night fell three times on the endlessly stretching waves, and when the fourth day dawned the ship was attacked by pirates. They ordered all the passengers to prepare their ransoms, and the deck of the ship was soon piled high with gold, silver, spices, silk, leather and wool. All the passengers were only too willing to add to the pile everything they had with them, but Abraham alone just stood and stared in front of him. "I was dogged by misfortune in Toledo," he thought to himself, "and things are no better here. How can I buy my freedom, when I have nothing?"

Most of the property belonged to one rich merchant. His servants brought three great chests: the first was full of pearls, the second of precious stones and the third of money. The rich man added his sumptuous robes, thinking to himself: "No one has such treasures as I. I shall surely be saved."

But the pirate chief thought otherwise. When the first passenger came up to him and offered his riches, the pirate replied: "It would be mine anyway." And he ordered his companions to throw the unfortunate fellow into the sea. The second and third passengers met the same fate, and it was not long before the rich merchant, too, had disappeared under the waves. The last person left on board was Abraham ibn Ezra.

"What will you give me for your life?" the pirate chief asked him. "As you can see, I am rich enough, and if you want to save your life, do not offer me gold."

"I have none to offer," said Abraham, softly. "I have nothing but my poems, songs, tales and riddles. It is all I possess."

The pirate replied, "I was able to say that everything aboard this ship belonged to me. But over your thoughts I have no power at all; therefore you may pay your ransom with them. Listen well: if you can give me a riddle which I cannot solve, you shall live. If not, I shall have you thrown into the sea like the others."

Abraham thought for a moment, and then said: "A battlefield without earth, a king without princes, a queen without robes, knights without horses, castles without windows. What is it?"

The pirate's brow furrowed; he thought about it all day and all night, but he could not solve the riddle. "We often pass the time on our long journeys with riddles," he said finally. "But I have never heard one as difficult as that. I give up."

"The battlefield without earth is a chessboard," said Abraham, "and the king, queen, knights and castles are pieces."

The pirate liked the riddle a lot. He gave orders at once that Abraham be taken ashore, and before releasing him he showered him with gifts. Abraham ibn Ezra recounted the tale of his salvation many times, but never forgot to add: "Cleverness is worth more than the greatest treasure. If you do not believe it, then try falling into the hands of pirates!"

Lunch
with the Lion

The lion invited all the animals to his place for lunch. At the appointed hour the animals filed into his parlor, and the lion showed each one where to sit. The last to arrive was the fox. Looking around him, he saw with horror that the roof of the lion's parlor was covered with the skins of dead animals. "Mighty king," said the fox to the lion with a bow, "might I be allowed to sing Your Majesty a song?"

"Please do," said the lion. "I shall be pleased to listen."

"And you animals," said the fox, turning to his fellow guests, "will surely not object to accompanying me?"

"We shall be glad to sing along with you," the animals replied.

"Then listen," said the fox, and he began: "What we see up there, is being prepared down here..."

The lion blissfully closed his eyes and marked time with a huge paw; but the animals did not fail to notice that the fox was looking up at the roof. They followed his gaze, and suddenly froze with horror. "Those poor creatures," they all realized, "were invited to lunch just like us — and look what happened to them! The lion killed them and skinned them!"

The animals began to slip silently away. The lion, engrossed in the song, did not even notice. Only when silence fell did he open his eyes. He was sitting alone in his parlor, and was just in time to see the fox disappearing in the distance. The fox then gathered the animals together and finished the song. "The mighty are not to be trusted," he sang. "They smile at you sweetly, but think only of themselves."

Vengeance in Vain

Abird who lived on the sea shore decided to build a nest. When the tide was out one day, he set to work. He fetched twigs, feathers and dry leaves, but no sooner had he gathered together everything he needed, than the tide came in. The waves rolled up and soon washed away everything the little bird had so carefully collected. The bird was furious. "I swear I shall take revenge on the sea!" he cried, and at once set about it. He took a drop of sea water in his beak, flew ashore, and emptied the water onto the ground. Then he picked up a beakful of sand and flew back to the sea with it. He dropped the sand in the sea, and flew back and forth like that until the moon came out. After a few days of this work, the little bird was quite exhausted. He sat on the shore watching the waves roll in, impatient to get his strength back so he could continue. Then another bird came flying up and said to him: "I have been watching you for a long time, and I am sorry for you. You wish to have your revenge, but vengeance is a poor counselor. Try as you may, you will never destroy the sea. But if you go to work with good intentions, even a little labor will have its reward."

The bird took his new friend's advice and flew inland, where he soon built a fine nest.

THE SIXTH LIGHT

The Ashkenazi Jews of Central and Eastern Europe

The Biter
Bit

Many years ago in Poland there was a certain poor trader. He had a houseful of children, but business was bad, so one day he said to himself that he might get on better in some foreign country. He gave his wife all the money he had left, took his leave of her and the children, and with a heavy heart set out into the world.

The tradesman passed through many countries, and made a profit everywhere he went. Just as misfortune had once dogged him, success now smiled on him. He bought and sold, and before the year was out he had 600 zloty jangling in the purse he kept under his shirt. "God has not forgotten me," he said to himself. "In a few months I have earned more than in the whole of my life." But then the tradesman remembered his wife and children, and his joy faded. He was so homesick, so longed to see them all again, that he could not take another step away from them. Selling all the goods he had, he set off homewards as fast as he could.

On his way home, he came one evening to the edge of a town. The Sabbath, when no devout Jew either works or travels, was approaching, so he quickly made preparations for the day. Close to one of the houses he dug a pit, and when he had washed in the river and put on his fresh Sabbath clothes he hid all his money in the hole, covered it with earth, and went off to the synagogue with a clear conscience.

The house near which the tradesman had hidden his money belonged to a certain old man. All who knew him took him for a pious and honest fellow, but there was greed concealed in his heart. He saw through his window how the stranger hid something in the ground, and as soon as the tradesman was gone the old man dug out the earth again. He found the purse containing the 600 zloty, and took it to his house.

When the Sabbath was over, the tradesman returned to his hiding place to find his money gone. Tears came to his eyes. "I have never before had enough to buy presents for my wife and children," he said to himself bitterly. "Now, when fortune has smiled on me, am I to lose everything again?" He looked around sadly, and noticed the nearby house. "Whoever lives in that house must have seen me hide my money," he thought to himself. "No one else could have seen me. But if I accuse him of theft, he will throw me out as a liar."

The tradesman pondered over what he should do. After a while he went and knocked on the door of the old man's house as if he knew nothing of the theft. "Peace be with you," he greeted the old man. "I am a stranger here, and I need advice. The people in the town spoke of your wisdom, which is why I have come to you. Be so kind as to hear what I have to say."

Flattered, the old man invited the tradesman in. "What is your wish?" he asked. "I will gladly help you if I can."

"I am trading in the countryside round about," the visitor told him. "Because I know no one here, and I am afraid of robbers, I have hidden a purse with six hundred zloty in a secret place. Now I do not know what I should do, for I have just received a further thousand zloty in payment of a debt, and I cannot decide whether I should hide the purse with the money in the ground, or entrust it to some honest man."

The old man smiled and said: "I could hide the money safely for you myself, but so that you may be sure I have no dishonest intentions, I'll tell you what to do. Bury the purse in the ground. Do it at night, so that no one can see you; the best thing would be for you to hide it in the same place as the 600 zloty. Since you are a stranger here, it would be better for you to have all your money in one place."

"I will do as you suggest," said the tradesman. "Thank you so much for your advice." He took his leave of the old man and quickly left his house.

As soon as the door had shut behind the tradesman, the old man hurried to fetch the purse with the 600 zloty. "The trader will go to put another thousand zloty in his hiding place," he thought. "And if he does not find his 600 zloty there, he will choose another place. I must return the first purse so when the trader buries another purse with a thousand zloty there I shall get all his money!"

As soon as dusk fell, the old man buried the purse with the 600 zloty in the place he had stolen it from. That was just what the tradesman had hoped he would do. Soon afterwards he came back and found his stolen money. There was not a single zloty missing.

"The old fellow wanted more, and now he has nothing," the tradesman said to himself with satisfaction. "Which is no more nor less than he deserves!"

He put the purse with the money back under his shirt, bought some fine presents, and the next Sabbath he spent in great joy back at home with his wife and children.

A Treasure in a Dream

In the Polish city of Cracow there once lived a rabbi called Eisik ben Jekel. He was a god-fearing and good man, but since his whole community was afflicted by poverty, the rabbi, too, was poor. Eisik ben Jekel always had some worry or other: with what was his wife to buy fish for the Sabbath? Where was he to get the money to repair the synagogue? How was he to pay for a new copy of the Torah? No sooner had Eisik solved one problem, than two more arose to take its place, and the rabbi would say bitterly that the only thing he was not short of was debts.

Poverty made Eisik ben Jekel sad, but it made his wife, Yenta, angry. "Eisik," she was always saying, "we have nothing to eat, and you simply wait for a miracle to happen. Do something! Elijah Hasofer was able to change the course of a river when he had to — why shouldn't God help you, too?"

Words like these made Eisik ben Jekel sadder than ever. How could he, an ordinary rabbi, compare with the wondrous sage Hasofer? When, many years before, the students of Cracow had, out of hatred for the Jews, hurled their children into the River Vistula, Elijah Hasofer had stood on the riverbank and ordered the river not to harm the children. The waters had obeyed: they had washed the children ashore, and carried away the wicked students instead. Thus the rabbi's learning and magic powers had saved the poor Jewish children, but Elijah Hasofer had not left it at that. Wishing to ensure their safety even after his death, he gave the river a further order, changing its course so that it no longer flowed close to the Jewish quarter.

Everyone in Cracow knew the story, but Eisik ben Jekel felt he lacked the powers of Elijah Hasofer. He did not know the secret books; his soul had never learned the wisdom of the highest celestial spheres. So Eisik did not reply to his wife's complaints; he only hoped that Yenta would take heart from his mysterious silence.

Year after year passed like that. But one winter Eisik had a strange dream several nights running. Each time an old man wearing a *streiml*, the large fur cap worn by the eastern Jews, appeared to him and said: "Eisik, go to Prague and dig beneath the bridge leading to the royal castle. You will find a treasure there."

Eisik was no great believer in dreams, but when the man appeared to him a fourth time, and a fifth, he decided he had better go to Prague. Taking a bundle containing a few essentials, he walked and walked until he spotted the towers of the Bohemian capital on the horizon. Eisik found the bridge leading to the royal castle, but when he saw it he felt a shock of disappointment. The bridge was a long one, and not only that, but it was guarded by a sentry. Even if the rabbi were to dig every day, he would surely have to spend several months in Prague. But he did not even start to dig — how could he without attracting the attention of the guard?

Rabbi Eisik ben Jekel spent long hours, soon whole days, on the bridge. From dawn till dusk he considered how he might fulfil the orders of the old man in his dream, but, try as he might, he could think of nothing. "That's what you get for relying on dreams,"

he finally said to himself in annoyance. "We are not all prophets, that we should believe in our visions."

Eisik turned about, and was just going to set off back to Cracow, when the sentry called him over. "I have been watching you for a long time," he told the rabbi, "and I should very much like to know why you are always dawdling on the bridge."

Eisik was in a dilemma. He did not want to tell his dream, but there was nothing else to do. He told the truth about why he had come to Prague, and the sentry burst out laughing. "How could you have been such a fool?" he guffawed, slapping his thighs with mirth. "If I were to believe in foolish dreams like that one, I should long ago have been in Cracow."

"Why? What did you dream of?" asked the rabbi, curiously.

"I dreamed I was to go to the house of a poor Jew named Eisik ben Jekel and dig beneath the stove," replied the sentry. "He is supposed to have a great treasure hidden there." The soldier paused for a moment and leaned towards Eisik confidentially. "Have you ever heard such nonsense? How could someone who owned a treasure be poor? And even if I believed there really was a treasure, how would I find this Eisik? I might as well dig up the whole city!"

When the sentry had finished speaking, Eisik ben Jekel set off home. He hurried as if he were fleeing death itself. Without even greeting his wife properly, he grabbed a spade and began to dig beneath the stove. Yenta looked on with dismay, but soon her anxiety turned to joy. The spade struck an iron-bound chest, and when the rabbi opened it the whole room shone with the glow of thousands of golden ducats.

From then on neither Rabbi Eisik ben Jekel nor his community was short of anything. He had a new synagogue built, and gave generously to all who were in need. His wife Yenta was satisfied, and she didn't mind in the least that her husband was not the great miracle-worker that Elijah Hasofer had been. Eisik devoted himself to holy studies until the day he died. He taught, explained the Scriptures, and gave a *drasha*, or Sabbath sermon, better than any in Cracow. "God is constantly helping us," Eisik ben Jekel would frequently say in his sermon. "But only He knows what is best for a man. Some He sends away from home to find their fortune, while others He sends out into the world only to show them that they are to seek their fortune under their own roofs. And that is how it was with me."

The Little
Judge

In the Polish town of Pinchow there once lived a rabbi called Ephraim who had a very clever son named Jonathan. Every day Jonathan went to the *cheder*, the Jewish school, returning home late in the afternoon. Pinchow was a small town with low houses and many dark little streets where scoundrels often prowled. One day, as Jonathan was hurrying to the cheder, he was accosted by a rough voice: "Where are you off to, little Jew? Don't you know how to say good day like a polite little boy?"

Standing in front of Jonathan was a giant of a man, reaching out a pair of huge hands. Jonathan knew who it was at once; it was Yatsek, a Polish horse-dealer, the terror of all the Jewish children. He liked nothing better than to hear them cry out with pain, so he beat them whenever he got the chance. Now he started beating Jonathan, throwing his books in the mud and not leaving the poor boy alone until he was covered in bruises. But Jonathan bore the pain bravely, and did not cry no matter how hard he was hit.

The horse-dealer had not expected such courage. "Why aren't you yelling and begging for mercy?" he growled. "Haven't you had enough?"

"Why should I yell?" replied Jonathan in a steady voice. "You have done what was necessary. Perhaps you do not know it, but today is a very special day. If one of your race beats a Jew, the Jew is obliged to thank him, and also to pay for the service. That is the age-old custom, so I beg you to accept these two coins from me. My mother gave them to me to buy my lunch with, but observing the law of our fathers is more important to me than having a piece of bread in my hand."

Yatsek's jaw sagged in astonishment. But there were indeed two shiny groschen lying in the boy's palm, so he believed the lad's cunning words. He took the money, turned on his heels and hurried to the town square. "Crazy Jews," he thought to himself. "They let themselves be beaten, and pay for it to boot. But if they are stupid, I am not. I shall wait for Jonathan's father, and he will pay for my blows in gold!"

That was exactly what Jonathan had hoped for. The greedy Yatsek was in for a surprise. The moment he laid hands on the rabbi, people gathered round him in fury, and Yatsek was led off to prison in chains. When he came before the court the simple-minded horse-dealer claimed he had only acted according to Jonathan's advice, but he did not escape just punishment. The Jewish children were now safe from the bully, who got only ridicule for his foolishness.

That evening Rabbi Ephraim said to his son, "You have judged, though you are not a judge, and you have used your wits to overcome the strong. My blessing be upon you."

It was not long afterwards that the peace of Pinchow was disturbed by a great quarrel. A certain Polish butcher accused his Jewish neighbor, a spice merchant, of stealing his money. It seemed at first sight to be a clear case of theft. The butcher described the purses, and said how many ducats were in each purse. Several witnesses said they had seen the purses at the butcher's, and soon after the theft was discovered the ducats were found at the house of the spice merchant.

But the Jew denied the accusation. "Our stalls are next to each other," he explained to the judge, "and are divided only by a thin wooden wall. The butcher watched me through a crack between the boards as I was counting my money, and that's how he knows what the purses look like and how much is in each. The whole town knows that my business is successful, but that only flies come to his stall. The money is mine, and the butcher's witnesses are lying."

The butcher at once began to shout that it had all been the other way around. "I was

the one who was counting my money," he swore. "And the spice merchant watched me through the wall. It is not enough that he is a thief, but he dares accuse me, an honest man, of stealing from him!"

The judge hesitated for a long time before giving his verdict, but it was plain to all that he would decide in favor of the butcher in the end. The spice merchant was likely to face a long prison sentence; all the Jews in Pinchow were subjected to the hatred of the Poles. At night their windows were broken, while in the daytime they were showered with insults.

In Rabbi Ephraim's house, the family talked all the time about the case. The rabbi was afraid that after judgement was passed the town would no longer be a safe place for the Jews, and he thought day and night about how he might help the spice merchant. He knew the man well, and did not doubt his word, but in order to save him he had to find proof of his innocence.

The day before the verdict was due to be brought, the rabbi was walking about his garden. Over and over again he pondered what he might do for the unfortunate Jew, but he couldn't think of anything. "Resign yourself to the will of God," he sighed at last. "There is nothing to do but leave town. Tomorrow may be too late."

Rabbi Ephraim went to fetch his son Jonathan, who was playing with some children not far from the house. The game was a peculiar one. One of the boys played the accused spice merchant, another the butcher who had lodged the complaint, while Jonathan played the part of the judge. The rabbi hid behind a tree and listened carefully to what the boys were saying. The boys who represented the conflicting parties defended themselves ferociously, hurling accusations; but then Jonathan spoke. "Hear the verdict!" he said in a clear tone of voice, as though he were not playing a game at all, but weighing the case on real scales of justice. "The ducats must be thrown into boiling water. If a greasy ring appears on the surface, then the Jew is a thief, and the money belongs to the butcher. The butcher's hands are always greasy, so his money must be greasy, too. But if the water remains clear, the money belongs to the spice merchant, and the butcher will be punished for making a false accusation."

The rabbi was astonished. He hurried to the judge's house. There he suggested that the trial he had just heard of should be made, and the judge agreed. The next day he had the money thrown into a pot of boiling water. When the servants took the pot off the fire and the surface became still, the water was clear, without a sign of fat. Now no one doubted the Jew's innocence. The avaricious butcher was found guilty, and the happy spice merchant was able to return home.

In the evening of that day the rabbi said to his son: "You have judged, though you are not a judge, and your wisdom has prevented a crime. May all your deeds be so blessed."

The rabbi's wish was fulfilled. When Jonathan grew up, he became a great man of learning, the support and comfort of his fellows. He traveled to many distant parts, and resolved many disputes; now he was face to face with the accused, and he was the acknowledged and universally respected moderator of the rabbinic court.

A Miraculous Feast

In Prague, the capital of Bohemia, there once lived many Jews. They occupied a large quarter of the city, and had several schools and synagogues there. In the middle of the Jewish quarter, near the River Vltava, stood the Old-New Synagogue. There was not another one like it in the whole world, for the angels themselves had helped to build it. They had brought the ruins of Solomon's temple from Jerusalem to Prague, and the synagogue had been raised on their foundations. But the Jewish schools of Prague were founded on the wisdom of their teachers. Many, many sages assembled there, the lights of Israel in her exile. And greatest of them all was the learned Jehuda Löw ben Bezalel.

Because he was so big and because of his great learning, they called him the high rabbi. He lived on the bank of the Vltava, in a house with a bunch of grapes carved in the stonework over the door. It was the sign of the descendants of the high priest Aaron, and a symbol which especially suited Rabbi Löw, for his wisdom was like the fruit of the vine. The largest and sweetest grapes grow close to the ground, and Rabbi Löw never tried to place himself above other men. He knew the secret arts and the mysteries of nature, and he wrote books of great merit, yet he did not grow proud. He helped all who needed advice, and even the emperor liked to hear what he had to say; he took a liking to Rabbi Löw, and would allow no harm to come to the Jews of Bohemia.

But the emperor's counselor set out to turn his master against Löw. The rabbi's learning afflicted him more than a wasting disease, and when he thought of the emperor asking the rabbi's advice, he turned pale with jealousy. There was nothing he yearned for more than for Löw to fall from the emperor's favor, so he devised a cunning plan. One day he went before the emperor and said: "Mighty ruler, it has become the custom for your ministers, generals and princes to hold great feasts in your honor. All have shown their loyalty in this manner, except for your confidant, Rabbi Löw. Who knows if he is not only exploiting your magnanimity?"

The wicked counselor knew well enough that Rabbi Löw had neither a splendid palace nor skilled cooks who could cater for an emperor's taste, but the emperor thought of one thing only – the rabbi did not respect him. So he summoned him at once and ordered him to hold a banquet in his honor within a week.

When the imperial counselor heard of the monarch's order, he rejoiced. He was sure it would be the ruin of Rabbi Löw, and he counted the days that remained until the banquet was to be held. On the appointed day a great crowd of people gathered round Rabbi Löw's house. Some had come to see the emperor with their own eyes, but there were also many who had been sent by the evil counselor. They wanted to be on the spot when the emperor's wrath was turned upon the rabbi and the other Jews, and in their black hearts they hoped they might be able to plunder the whole of the Jewish quarter.

At long last the emperor's coach came rumbling along the paving stones, with a long train of courtiers behind. Rabbi Löw went out to meet his emperor. "Gracious Majesty," he said with a bow, "I am glad to be able to welcome you and your court to my banquet. Be so kind as to follow me." Rabbi Löw set off upstream along the Vltava, and before long the emperor saw a magnificent castle. None of his subjects could remember it being there before, and the imperial counselor, who had been looking forward to his triumph, caught his breath.

"Please come in," Rabbi Löw invited the emperor and his entourage. "I have prepared a feast such as no monarch has been honored with before."

The rabbi had spoken the truth. The castle he led his guests into was built all of marble. The furniture was carved out of rare exotic woods, the floors were covered with thick oriental carpets, and everywhere they looked there were ornaments of pure gold and silver. The dining-hall where the banqueting table stood was larger than the most spacious hall in the imperial palace. On the long table there was a snow-white tablecloth; the handles of the cutlery were set with precious stones, and behind each chair stood a servant whose livery was embroidered with gold.

The emperor was greatly impressed by his reception, and his enthusiasm grew when he tasted the first dishes. He and his courtiers were delighted with the fine flavor of each course, enthralled with the wines they were offered; the only one of the guests who was not pleased was the imperial counselor. Whether he had in his mouth crisp roast meat or a sweet dessert, it had a bitter taste, but through no fault of the cooks. He sat throughout the banquet in stubborn silence, and each word of praise the emperor had for Rabbi Löw stung him more than a swarm of bees.

When, late that night, the feast was over, the emperor thanked Rabbi Löw in front of all the guests, and the courtiers, too, were full of praise for their host. As they rose to make their way back to the palace, the emperor noticed that his counselor had remained seated. "What are you waiting for?" he asked him. "The banquet is over, and you, who most wished to turn me against the rabbi, do not wish to leave him now?"

The counselor rolled his eyes and fidgeted, then mumbled unhappily, "I can't get up. Some sort of power is holding me to my chair."

Everyone was amazed, and the emperor asked the rabbi to explain. "It's simple," said Rabbi Löw. "This man has stolen the golden goblet from which he was drinking his wine. Until he returns it, he will not be able to leave the castle."

The counselor tried once more to leave the table but to no avail. In the end he had to admit the theft. He drew the missing goblet from a fold in his garments, and the moment he placed it on the table the spell was broken. Red with shame, the counselor stood up, and in a shaky voice begged the emperor's forgiveness. But the monarch did not even allow him to finish what he was saying. "Get out of my sight!" he shouted. "I have already seen that you have a mean tongue, but now I know that you also have greedy fingers!"

The wicked counselor left with his head hung low, and never dared show his face at court again. He wandered through the world, wondering how Rabbi Löw had come by a splendid castle, and in particular how he had discovered the theft of the goblet. The emperor, too, was anxious to learn the solution to those mysteries. And it was not long before an explanation was forthcoming.

Shortly after the banquet given by Rabbi Löw, a messenger from a distant land was announced at the imperial palace. When the emperor received him, he learned that the king of the far-off country had prepared a celebration for the occasion of a particularly great holiday. He had invited many sovereigns, princes and princesses, and had had a fabulous marble castle built; then he had ordered dozens of the finest cooks to prepare exquisite foods for the banquet. On the appointed day the guests had arrived, but as they were about to enter the castle, it had moved. It had risen high above the clouds and disappeared into the distance, like a feather blown in the wind. The next day the castle had returned, but all the food had been eaten and all the wine drunk.

At that moment the emperor understood everything. Rabbi Löw had brought the castle with his supernatural powers, and had cast a spell on everything in it, so that nothing might be lost. From then on the emperor respected the rabbi more than ever, and made him his most intimate advisor.

How Rabbi Löw
Made the Golem

It is written in the sacred books of the Jews that before God sent the children of Israel into exile, he made a covenant with them and with the other nations. The Jews promised they would not try to return to the Holy Land before God himself led them there, and that they would not rise up against the nations among which they were to live. The other nations gave their word that they would not oppress the Jews. The covenant was signed, God set his seal upon it, and the Jews dispersed throughout the whole world. Wherever they went, they kept their part of the bargain. They were glad of the hospitality they received, kept the laws of their ancestors, and waited patiently for the return to their homeland. But the nations which surrounded the Jews of Moses always had among them those who broke the covenant. Wicked people hated the Jews, and accused them of all sorts of things. The streets of the Jewish quarters and their synagogues were more than once stained with the blood of the innocent, and those who survived these onslaughts forgot each tribulation only when its memory was supplanted by one even more painful.

"Lord," lamented the Jews throughout the world, "are we to remain forever without assistance? Is there no one who will save us?" The wise and just Rabbi Löw of Prague heard these complaints, and once when a wave of hatred against his brothers was sweeping through Bohemia, he decided to do something. He asked God in a dream how he might avert the threat of disaster, and God replied: "Make a *golem*, a body of clay, and bring it to life. The golem will protect the Jews from all their enemies."

The next morning Rabbi Löw summoned his son-in-law, Isaac ben Samson, and the best of his pupils, Jacob ben Haim Sasson, from the priestly tribe of Levites. "I have brought you here," he told them, "because I need your help. We have already been subjected to enough injustice. Therefore I will make a powerful golem, a creature neither good nor evil, but obedient to my every command. According to the ancient arts and the secret books all four elements must be present; you Isaac, will represent fire, Jacob will symbolize water, and I shall be air. The only one left is earth, and when we have made perfect preparations for our task, God will show us where to find that."

The three men spent the next few days in contemplation and prayer. Rabbi Löw also studied the book of wonders written by Abraham, father of the Jewish nation; it is a book full of secret symbols, where letters are counted like numbers and numbers can be read

like letters. When seven days had passed, Rabbi Löw saw the banks of the River Vltava in a dream. The spot which appeared to him was covered with fine, freshly washed-up clay, and on its surface was the outline of a body. He called his assistants at once. It was exactly midnight, on the second day of the month of Adar. First the men went to the *mikveh*, the cleansing baths, and then, dressed in the white robes worn on holidays, they made for the Vltava. In their hands they held candles, the only lights in a darkness which hid even the moon and the stars.

When Rabbi Löw found the place he had seen in his dream, he told his companions to begin reading the Psalms. Then he drew in the earth the outline of a huge human body, pressed in the nose, ears, mouth and eyes, and marked the fingers and toes. The golem lay on its back motionless, like a man deep in slumber.

The rabbi turned to Isaac ben Samson. "You are *esh*, fire. Walk seven times round the golem from right to left." He leaned towards his son-in-law and whispered in his ear a miraculous formula understood only by the initiated, and Isaac set off. He walked around the clay figure, repeating in a quavering voice the words made up of magic syllables. When he circled the golem the first time, the body began to dry out. As he passed the head a third time, the golem began to give off warmth. At the fifth circle it came aglow, and at the seventh it was as hot as a furnace.

Then Rabbi Löw addressed Jacob Haim ben Sasson. "You are *mayyim*, water," he told him. "Walk seven times round the golem from left to right." Jacob set off walking around the figure in the opposite direction to that taken by Isaac, also reciting a spell which the rabbi had whispered to him. As he passed the head for the first time, the clay figure lost its ruddy glow. As he passed it for the third time, steam began to rise from the golem, and its body grew moist. At the fifth time hair grew on the clay head, and nails grew on the fingers and toes, and at the seventh circle the body became covered with skin.

Then Rabbi Löw himself, representing air, walked around the golem. He went first in one direction, then the other, and finally placed in the golem's mouth a slip of parchment on which the ineffable name of God was written. The men then bowed to east, west, south and north, and spoke the words of God's teaching together: "And the Lord God made man from the dust of the earth, and breathed life into his nostrils."

The moment the word life crossed their lips, the golem sat up. Fire, water and air had roused his earthen body, and now he looked around for the first time. "Rise!" Rabbi Löw ordered him. The golem obeyed, and its creator told it: "Your name is Joseph. I have created you to protect the Jews from all danger, and you will obey my every command. If I send you into fire, you will go. If I order you to throw yourself from a cliff or to jump into the depths of the ocean, you will do so!"

The golem nodded to show that he understood, but he could not reply. He was created by a man, not by God, so that the divine light in him was veiled. But otherwise the golem did not differ from a man. When the rabbi gave him the clothes he had brought with him, and showed him how to put them on, the golem looked like a servant from the synagogue. And that was how Rabbi Löw introduced him to his wife, Perl. The golem was given a small room in Rabbi Löw's house, and he obediently followed all his creator's instructions.

Most of the time the golem walked the streets of the Jewish quarter by day and by night to make sure no one tried to harm its inhabitants. Anyone who came to the Jews with bad intentions did so at his own risk, for the golem, a creature without flesh and bones, had an ability no man possesses. His soul felt more free in that body of clay, so that he knew exactly when the healing fragrances of Paradise came to earth. He would inhale them all, and this gave him a strength which no mortal could resist. He could be neither slain nor wounded, and like animals, demons and spirits he saw things that were hidden from human eyes. When necessary, Rabbi Löw gave him an amulet which made him invisible; he was able to creep secretly into the houses of enemies and find out about their plots against the Jews. He would then find Rabbi Löw and with gestures warn him of their intentions, and the wise rabbi knew at once what steps to take to avert the danger.

Thus it was that the Jews at last received their long-awaited defender. Only three men knew how he had arrived in Prague, but thousands were grateful to him for their peace of mind.

The Golem
Lends a Hand

From the day the golem made his appearance in Prague, the Jews there were safer than if they had been protected by the strongest of fortifications. The enemies of the people of Moses soon found that they were powerless against such an adversary, and as their intrigues began to grow less frequent, the golem had less and less work to do. He now kept watch only at night; in the daytime he would serve in the synagogue, but he would also spend long hours sitting in front of the rabbi's house. Rabbi Löw's wife Perl didn't approve of this. She had seven children to look after, and didn't know whether she was standing on her head or her heels, and there was the golem just twiddling his thumbs and sunning himself. But the rabbi had told his wife quite plainly: "Don't give the golem housework to do!" So Perl had to do everything herself, though she often wondered why it was she was not allowed to make use of the golem.

Once, just before the feast of Pesach, Perl had more work than ever. At Pesach the Jews eat only unleavened bread, such as their forefathers took with them when they were led out of Egyptian bondage. Nothing which has been fermented must be left in the house, so Perl had to scrub the floors and sweep up, so that not even a crumb of ordinary bread might be left lying about. She also had to do the shopping and cooking, and get ready the special vessels which are used only for Pesach. She did not stop working from morning till night, and one day when she saw the golem lounging on the bench she said, "I've had enough of this! God knows, I have never asked the golem to do anything, but this time I need his help. It can't matter just this once!"

Perl called the golem and said, "I am going to the market, and I want you to bring water in while I'm gone. Here you have two buckets: the well is in the yard."

The golem nodded, and the moment the door closed behind the rabbi's wife, he went hurrying into the yard. Perl was glad to be saved some of her work, but when, after a while, she returned from the market, she threw up her hands in horror. A crowd of people had gathered on her doorstep, and a stream of water was pouring out of the door, as if a spring had erupted in Rabbi Löw's house. "A flood!" the people cried. "A flood is beginning!"

Suddenly the familiar voice of the rabbi was heard above the hubbub. "Nothing of the sort," he said. He had just come home for his lunch, and had been watching for a good while. "God sent the flood upon mankind to punish them for their sins, but this is only a punishment for my disobedient wife."

It was only then that Perl spotted the golem. Soaked with water from head to foot, he came running into the house, emptied both buckets in the passage, and dashed straight back to the well. In an instant he had refilled the buckets and was hurrying back towards the door.

"Joseph, stop bringing water!" called Rabbi Löw.

The golem stopped at once. He put the buckets down on the floor and went back to his seat as if nothing had happened. The people went away, leaving the rabbi and his wife alone in the yard. "It is written," said the rabbi, "that vessels set aside for sacred uses are not to be used for everyday purposes. It is the same with the golem. We may use him for godly ends, but not otherwise."

From that day on Perl was careful not to ask the golem to do anything. She did all the work herself with the help of her daughters, though there was another helper growing up in the house. Many years previously Rabbi Löw had adopted a little orphan girl, and as she grew older Perl was able to rely on her more and more. But the day came for the girl to get married. Rabbi Löw got her a dowry, and his wife began to make ready a marriage feast. There was a terrible amount of work to do. Perl hurried to and fro in the kitchen, and kept needing things fetching, but if there had been fifty pairs of hands in the house it wouldn't have been enough.

The only one who was doing nothing was the golem. He sat on the bench with his head in his hands, and did not seem too happy himself that he was so inactive. Perl thought to herself, "Marrying off a daughter is a godly business – why shouldn't I send the golem to do a little shopping?"

The rabbi's wife took some money and pushed it into the golem's hand, saying: "Joseph, down by the river there lives an old fisherman. Buy a big fish from him and bring it to me. After that you can go to the market for some apples." She gave him two slips of paper on which it was written what the fisherman and the market-woman were to give him, and the golem set off.

He arrived at the fisherman's at the right moment. The old man had just caught a huge carp, and was happy to sell it to the golem. But the golem had neither basket nor bag to put it in. At first he stood there helplessly, holding the fish between his enormous palms, but then he had an idea. Drawing his belt in tight, he shoved the fish into his shirt, and hurried home.

The fish he was carrying was a truly fine specimen. Its head was on the golem's stomach, but its tail reached up to his head. It twisted and turned so violently that the golem was scarcely able to keep hold of it, and then suddenly brought him such a sharp blow on the chin with its tail that it sent him reeling. Joseph lost his temper. He grabbed hold of the carp and gave it a good shake, as if to teach it a lesson, and then threw it in a broad arc right back into the Vltava.

The golem arrived home empty-handed. "Didn't you find the fisherman?" Perl asked him.

Joseph began to gesticulate wildly. He showed the rabbi's wife what the mischievous fish had done to him, and how he had punished it. Perl didn't know whether to laugh or be angry. But it was nearly time for the wedding feast to begin, so she let the golem be and hurried out to buy another fish.

The golem, too, went out again. Perl had given him two things to do — to get a fish and to get some apples — so he set off for the market-place. He found a stall selling apples straight away. Giving the woman the piece of paper the rabbi's wife had provided him with, he waited until she weighed out the apples. But then he went on standing there, thinking the bag of apples was too small.

"What are you waiting for?" asked the market-woman, mockingly. "Do you want the whole stall?"

The golem nodded, and bent down. He lifted up the whole stall, along with the apples and the woman, and, setting it on his shoulders, hurried back to the rabbi's house. The woman yelled and shrieked as though the devil were carrying her off to hell; the golem panted and wheezed, and a crowd of people ran alongside them, gathering up the fallen apples. Perl was already back from the fisherman's, and the golem made straight towards her. He put the stall down in the yard next to the well, and when he had dragged the half-dead market-woman out from under the apples, he looked proudly at the rabbi's wife, as if expecting high praise.

The affair caused quite a sensation in the city, and the apple-woman was only mollified when the rabbi and his wife invited her to the wedding feast. From then on Rabbi Löw had no need to be anxious lest his wife should make use of the golem's services. Joseph only ate and slept in the house, and no one asked him to do any work again.

In time it became apparent that the golem was no longer needed to keep watch over the Jewish quarter in Prague. The attacks and slanders against its inhabitants had dwindled almost to nothing, and Rabbi Löw saw that there was no longer any call for a golem in Bohemia. He summoned Isaac ben Samson and Jacob Haim ben Sasson to the attic of the Old-New Synagogue to return the golem to the earth from which he came. They did this in exactly the same way as they had brought him to life, except that everything was the other way round.

First they spoke the words about the creation of man, but backwards. Rabbi Löw then took from the golem's mouth the piece of parchment bearing the ineffable name of God, and each of the men walked round the figure seven times. Isaac ben Samson, who had walked from right to left when the golem was created, now walked from left to right, and Jacob Haim ben Sasson went from right to left. They pronounced the magic syllables in the reverse order, and finally Rabbi Löw did the same. The elements of fire, water and air left the golem, and when, after midnight, the three men stepped out into the winding streets of the sleeping city, they left behind them only lifeless earth. Rabbi Löw spread the word that his servant Joseph had left Prague, and strictly forbade anyone to go into the attic of the Old-New Synagogue.

✡

Pinkas
and the Count

Long, long ago, there lived in the Jewish quarter of Prague a second-hand dealer called Pinkas. He bought and sold everything imaginable, dealt in anything he could lay his hands on, but his life was not an easy one. Whether he had more to sell or less, he never made more than a few groschen, so he and his wife and children often went to bed on empty stomachs.

But once a week at least Pinkas was able to look after his family properly. Since he was a righteous man and well-versed in the wisdom of his forefathers, he found favor with a certain wealthy count. The nobleman did not mind that Pinkas was only a poor shopkeeper: he liked to talk with him, and would help him in return. When the holy Sabbath drew near, he gave him money to buy flour, fish, wine and candles, and at other feasts, too, he remembered his protégé.

Pinkas was a truly pious man. He never missed his prayers, and observed the sacred teaching in everything he did. When there was nothing to eat, he would say, "If the potter wants to test his wares, he taps a strong jug, not a weak one. Thanks be to God for subjecting me to the trials of the just." When he received his usual gift from the count, he would repeat the words of the psalm: "The lion cubs suffer privation and hunger, but they who seek the Lord want for nothing that is good. Thanks be to God for taking such good care of me."

The count was fond of Pinkas, but it irked him that he had never shown any gratitude in so many years. "If it were not for my money," he would say to himself, "Pinkas would have a lean time of it on feast days. But it is always God he gives thanks to, never me."

So it came about that the count grew annoyed with Pinkas, and by and by his annoyance turned to anger. One day he came to the end of his patience. When Pinkas came to him for money so that he might celebrate the feast of Pesach, he said, "My dear Pinkas, the gift you received from me at the last Sabbath was the last you will get. Since you always give praise to God for His providence, I have decided that you do not need me. Your God will surely help you, and I hope you will recall in times of abundance the exodus of the Jews from Egyptian bondage."

Pinkas felt sad. It was no small matter to buy things for the feast of Pesach, and now, with the start of the holiday only a week away, he hadn't even enough money to buy dry bread. As soon as his wife heard the news, she burst into tears. She lamented the

misfortune that had befallen them, and the wretched Pinkas took his sack of wares to see if he could sell something at the last moment. But he did not make a farthing, either that day or the next.

When darkness fell Pinkas gazed anxiously at the moon. The full moon which marked the beginning of the feast of Pesach was drawing close, and he still had no idea how they were going to get by. With a sigh, he took down his holy books and sought relief from his troubles in their wisdom.

It was two days before Pesach, and Pinkas was engrossed in the sacred books, when a loud noise disturbed the peace in his house. A heavy object crashed through the window of the room where he was sitting, and landed at his feet. He heard a wicked laugh from the street outside, as if the Devil himself had come visiting. Then all was silent again. Pinkas looked down at the floor and saw, lying amidst the broken glass, a dead monkey.

When the tradesman had recovered a little from the shock, he went and woke his wife. The two of them examined the monkey, and began to shake with fear. The ornate collar showed that the animal belonged to some rich man.

"What are we to do?" wailed Pinkas' wife. "Whoever threw the monkey in here may call the guard. No one will believe that we did not steal the creature and kill it, and all the Jews will suffer on our account."

But Pinkas did not lose his head. "We'll get rid of the monkey," he said, "and nothing will happen to us. The best thing would be for us to burn it in the stove."

Instructing his wife to get the fire going, Pinkas picked the monkey up by the tail. He was surprised to find he could scarcely carry it. "Who would have thought such a small creature would weigh more than a sack of stones," he gasped. With a struggle he carried the monkey to the stove, and then there was a jingling sound like that of coins falling on the floor.

Pinkas stopped dead in surprise. He turned to see where the noise was coming from, and there was another clink on the floor. Then a whole pile of gold ducats poured out of the animal's mouth.

"Wife!" cried Pinkas, in excitement. "God has not forgotten us! We are rich!"

Neither the tradesman nor his wife had ever seen so much money. They cleaned one coin after another and placed them in a special purse. Then they burned the monkey so thoroughly that not a whisker remained. Before the flames in the stove had died down, Pinkas' wife knew exactly what she would buy the next day: new clothes for herself and the children, festive crockery and food for the table, as the ancient custom required.

The next day was the happiest of Pinkas' life. Though he had scarcely a couple of ducats less in the purse at the end of it, his house changed beyond all recognition. The joiners brought in new furniture, and the whole place had a holiday air about it. In the evening Pinkas returned from the synagogue. He sat down at the head of the table, and when he had given his blessing the ceremonial eve of Pesach began.

The aroma of roast meat came drifting in from the oven, and goblets of red wine stood on the shining white tablecloth. In the centre of the table stood a large dish. It contained unleavened bread, a bone roast in ash, a mixture of apples, almonds and nuts, boiled eggs, watercress, horseradish and a bowl of salt water. Each of these foods was a reminder of the trials of the Jews in Egypt. Pinkas then read about them in his Haggadah, a well-thumbed book passed on to him by his father, and about the glorious deliverance of pharaoh's slaves, and the retribution wrought upon the cruel ruler and his armies.

Pinkas had just finished reading, with particular emotion, a prayer in praise of the goodness and might of God, when someone knocked on the window. At once the door opened, and into the room stepped the count. He looked around in astonishment. "Either you were never poor at all, or you have grown rich overnight," he said to Pinkas. "I came to see how you were celebrating Pesach, but I did not expect such luxury as this."

"Noble sir," replied Pinkas, "you have always seen to my well-being, so I shall tell you the truth. Heaven itself came to my assistance." And he told the astounded aristocrat the story of the monkey with the ducats in its stomach; the count grew more and more amazed as he spoke.

"Did the monkey have a collar?" he asked when the dealer had finished.

Pinkas nodded his head, and described the monkey's collar.

The count began to laugh. "I should never have believed such a thing possible," he said. Shaking his head in disbelief, he went on, "The monkey which brought you such wealth, Pinkas, would, until a few days ago, sit on my shoulder. It saw me often as I tested golden ducats between my teeth, and the poor creature must have thought I was eating them. It probably ate so many of them that it died. But neither I nor anyone else knew of its taste for gold. So I had no hesitation in having it disposed of, and unknown to myself, my servant seems to have played a wicked trick on you. He threw the monkey's body through your window, and it is to his malice that you owe your treasure."

Pinkas was horrified. He brought the purse with the remaining ducats at once, promising to repay those he had spent, even if it meant selling his house. But the count shook his head. "I want nothing from you," he told Pinkas. "When I used to give you presents, I did not like to hear you thanking God, and not me. But you were right. Now I see for myself that my money goes straight to you even without my giving it, and I cannot set myself against the will of God."

The monkey filled with ducats brought good fortune to the second-hand dealer's house. Pinkas soon gave up his former trade and began to deal in better things, and by the next Pesach his money would no longer fit in a single purse. He never had to take the count's charity again, and visited him only when the nobleman wished to talk with him. But Pinkas never forgot what poverty was. He looked after the poor as if they were his own children, remaining as righteous and as pious as ever. Thus it was that in the course of time he became the head of all the Jews of Prague. He managed their affairs with wisdom and justice, and towards the end of his life had a new synagogue built. It stands in Prague to this day, and is named after Pinkas.

The Wolf
and the Animals

Once upon a time the wolf was put on trial for his cruelty. "Sire," the animals complained to the lion, "we cannot live with the wolf any longer. Wherever he goes, he leaves behind only destruction, death and lamentation. His thirst for blood makes widows of our wives and orphans of our children. Help us, we beseech you!"

The lion was very angry. "No punishment is too great for you," he thundered at the wolf. "Yet no matter how much I could make you suffer, it would not bring the dead back to life. But you will not be so cruel in future. For a whole two years from this day you may not kill a single creature. You must consider your guilt, and eat only animals which you find dead."

The wolf promised the lion that for two years he would not kill a single animal, and went his way. But it was not long before he caught sight of a lamb, grazing contentedly. He felt an overwhelming desire to taste warm blood. "What am I to do?" he pondered. "Am I to go two years without fresh meat? But my vow is important, I cannot break it just like that." The wolf shuffled his feet nervously, until suddenly he had an idea. "What is a year?" he said to himself. "365 days. And what is a day? Day is when I see. When I do not see, it is night. If I close my eyes, I see nothing, and it is night. If I open them, I can see; therefore it is day."

The wolf began to open and close his eyes quickly, carefully counting as he did so: "Open, shut — one day; open, shut — two days." He went on like that until he had counted 730 days, or two years. Then he cried, "I have fulfilled my promise to the lion! Two years have passed, and in all that time I have not killed a living creature." And he pounced on the lamb and ate it.

A scoundrel cannot be trusted: he will always find a way round a promise.

Who Is Better?

One day the forest trees started laughing at the fruit trees. "How feeble you are!" they jeered. "You are like dwarfs, and when the wind blows your rustle can scarcely be heard. See how tall and graceful we are, and how loudly our branches roar in the wind!"

"You have nothing to boast about," the fruit trees replied. "Though we are small and our crowns are not as fine as yours, people like us even better than you. They care for us and tend us, because we give them tasty fruit. You stretch yourselves up and show off your beauty, but what use is that when no one wants your fruit?"

✡

THE SEVENTH LIGHT

The Hasids

The Light
of Hanukka

Many, many years ago, there lived in Mesiborzi in Poland a certain Rabbi Baruch, grandson of the famous Baal-shem-tov. Like his grandfather, he was a *tzaddik* — an extraordinary man, a saint of saints and a true worker of miracles. The words of Baruch reached the very throne of God, and he knew how to serve the Creator with song and dance. When he prayed he set all seven heavens quivering, and when he rejoiced, the angels, too, were joyful. For this reason people came from all around to be with him. Since the time of Baal-shem-tov those who had their own tzaddik had been called *hasids*, and Rabbi Baruch, like his grandfather, helped and advised his hasids.

Rabbi Baruch was especially good at explaining the mysteries of the Torah, the sacred book of the Jews. The spark of God burned in him, and would ignite the souls of his pupils like a true fire. They clung to each word the tzaddik spoke, wanting to know and understand everything. Rabbi Baruch loved all his hasids for this, but Israel, son of a poor blacksmith, was his favorite. What a boy he was! His eyes shone like the eyes of an angel, and there was no pupil sharper or more quick-witted than he.

One autumn day Israel decided he would go home to visit his father. Rabbi Baruch was loath to part with his best-loved pupil, but Israel assured his teacher he would return for Hanukka, the feast of lights, so the rabbi gave him his blessing and the boy set off.

The three months Israel spent at his father's house passed like a week. A cold spell came, and snow fell, and Israel harnessed his horses to return to his tzaddik. It was only two days before the feast of Hanukka was to begin, and Israel could hardly wait to take his seat beside Rabbi Baruch at the festive table. Leaping onto the sleigh, he drove his horses across the snow-decked plains until, as twilight fell, he reached a large inn.

Israel reined in his horses. "If I sleep here," he thought, "I shall reach the rabbi's house tomorrow evening. But if I drive on without rest, I shall hear his voice at morning prayers." The young man was frozen stiff and his whole body ached from the long ride, but the thought that he would soon see his teacher gave him strength. With a crack of the whip, the sleigh lunged forward, and the lights of the inn were soon left far behind.

Israel drove on and on; he looked neither to the right nor the left, but tore through the snow as fast as he could. It was now quite dark. Suddenly a strong wind rose, extin-

guishing the lamp Israel was using to light his way and sweeping snow into his eyes. The lad had no notion where the horses were taking him; he had to summon all his strength to prevent the storm from tearing him from the sleigh. Suddenly, the horses stopped; the sleigh came to a standstill with a bump, and before Israel knew what was happening strong hands had taken hold of him. His sleigh had fallen into the hands of robbers.

Poor Israel had no idea that he had gone astray, and driven into a place surrounded by tall, deep forests filled with bandits. The robbers took the sleigh into the depths of the forest and began to examine their booty. They were convinced that Israel must be the son of a rich merchant, but search as they might, they could not find a farthing.

They were just about to fling themselves angrily upon Israel to punish him for being penniless, when the biggest of them called out: "Keep him alive; who knows, he might have been on his way to dig up a hidden treasure! It would be a pity to lose it. Let us take him to our leader — he can get any secret out of anybody!"

The robbers laughed. "A good idea," they said, "we'll do as you suggest." They blindfolded Israel and tied him to the sleigh, and the big fellow took the reins. He drove the sleigh along secret tracks known only to the robbers, skirting the edges of precipitous slopes. Now Israel wished he had spent the night in the inn, but it was too late for such thoughts. The robbers drove deeper and deeper into the forest, and all notions of escape were in vain.

It was a long time before the sleigh stopped. An unknown hand tore the blindfold from Israel's eyes, and the boy saw in front of him a large hut surrounded by huge trees. Dawn had broken, but the dense branches of the trees let through so little light that it seemed like dusk. In a while a shaggy figure wrapped in furs emerged from the hut. All four fingers of his left hand were missing, and a crimson scar stretched right across his forehead. "I am the robber chief," he told Israel in a deep, gruff voice, "and I want to know where you were going and why."

Israel was not afraid. He began to explain that he was a pupil of Rabbi Baruch, and that he had been hurrying back to him for the feast of Hanukka; but the robber chief interrupted him. "Do you expect me to believe your fairy tales?" he asked. "No one goes visiting in the middle of the night even in summer, let alone in a snowstorm! Tell the truth! Where did you hide the treasure? Where is the money?"

"There is no treasure in the whole world greater than that which Rabbi Baruch carries in his heart," replied Israel, quietly. "Believe me, I desire nothing more than to be close to him, which is why I was traveling by night. He who looks at the tzaddik, sees with new eyes. He who has not heard his voice remains deaf."

The robber chief lost his temper. He beat the boy with a stick, questioned him all day, but to no avail. Israel only repeated over and over that he had hidden no money, and kept talking about the wondrous power of his rabbi and the strength of his thoughts.

"I have heard enough," the robber chief said finally in disgust. "You must be crazy, and it is a pity to waste time on such as you. I shall let you go: you may drive where you will. The forest is deep, mark you, and full of danger. If your horses put a foot wrong you will plunge into a chasm. The wolves are hungry, and hunt everything that moves. Believe me, you will not leave the forest alive!"

The robbers sat Israel on his sleigh and took him a good distance away from their hideout. Then they disappeared suddenly, as though the ground had swallowed them up. The boy was alone. Tall trees rose all around him, and deep drifts covered the ground. There was a heavy silence, broken only by the distant howling of wolves. Darkness was falling once more, bringing with it the start of the feast of Hanukka. Tears came to Israel's eyes. "I wanted to get to the rabbi as soon as possible," he said, bitterly, "and instead robbers have beaten me and left me alone in a strange forest. How am I to get out again? Who will help me?"

As Israel was growing desperate, Rabbi Baruch was gathering his pupils in his house. Evening prayers were over, and each was sitting in his place. Only one chair was empty. "Israel has not come for the holiday," the rabbi thought sadly. "Has he forgotten his promise, or has he met with some misfortune?" Deep in thought, he stepped over to the eight-branched candelabrum, the *hanukkiya*, and lit the first light. "*Hanerot halalm*," he began to sing, that song in praise and thanks to their courageous forebears who had long ago defeated a cruel enemy and cleaned out the desecrated temple. But at that moment the flame flickered and suddenly went out.

The pupils leapt to their feet in alarm. One tried to relight the candle, but the rabbi motioned him to sit down. He stood at the head of the table, pale and lost in concentration. His sight dimmed. Then, suddenly, his face lit up and he told them: "Do not grieve, but celebrate the feast as it should be celebrated. I know the flame will return."

All this time Israel stayed where the robbers had left him. It was so dark he could not see a single pace in front of him, and the howling of the wolves was getting nearer and nearer. The horses were shaking with fear, and even if he had whipped them, they would not have taken a step from that place. But the boy had no thought of moving anyway. He sat hunched up on the sleigh with his eyes closed, saying his prayers.

All of a sudden he felt a soft, warm touch on his cheek. He straightened up in surprise — and cried out with joy. A short distance away from him a small flame was dancing, as if someone were holding up an invisible candle. The flame moved from side to side in front of the sleigh, and not even the strongest gusts of wind were able to blow it out. The horses set off after it. The flame meandered among the trees, lighting the way more clearly than a flaming brand. Wolves fled from its light, and soon their voices were no longer to be heard. As soon as the sleigh emerged from the forest, Israel urged his horses on. The sleigh glided across the snow as if it had sprouted wings, and the flame preceded it like some bright star. At long last the house of Rabbi Baruch came into view. When he arrived there, Israel leapt down from the sleigh, and the moment he opened the door the candle of the hanukkiya lit up.

The pupils were dumbfounded. They gathered round the rabbi, but he was unsurprised, for he was a saint, who saw things that were hidden from other human beings. He greeted Israel, and then the young man recounted his tale. It was only then that the pupils understood where the light of the hanukkiya had gone to, and to what Israel owed his salvation. They gave thanks to God for His assistance, and praised the wisdom of Rabbi Baruch. They sang and rejoiced until daybreak, and ate the cheese pastries which are baked only at Hanukka. Israel had never tasted better ones, nor did he ever eat food with more gratitude to the end of his life.

The Goat
with Human Eyes

Not far from the town of Kotsk in Poland there once lived a hosier named Leib. He got up every day at dawn so he could knit three pairs of stockings by lunchtime, and when he had finished them he took them to market in town. By evening he had always sold the stockings, and was able to buy new wool, so that the next morning at daybreak he was able to start work again. So it went on, day after day and year after year. There was no time for anything else, so Leib remained without learning. He could neither read nor write, and he had never heard the Torah explained. This troubled him greatly. "I am old," he said, "but my children could teach me to read. Otherwise when I die I shall not even be able to read the judgement of the heavenly court."

But Leib had one joy in his life, his tobacco box. When he paused from his work for a moment to take out a little tobacco and have a smoke, the world seemed a much happier place. His eyes lit up and his fingers grew warm, as if he had taken a drink of the water of life. Leib bought himself new tobacco every week, and he always used it up to the last strand.

One evening as he returned with his tobacco box full, he whistled contentedly, and his heart was as light as a feather. He was happy that he had made a little more money than usual, and was looking forward to a nice smoke. He smiled at the moon, and not even his lack of learning mattered to him as much as usual. But before the next hour struck Leib was filled with dismay. As soon as he got home he put his hand in his pocket, and found that his tobacco box was no longer there. Taking a lantern, he hurried out of the house and searched the length and breadth of every street he had passed along, but in vain: the box had vanished altogether.

Leib burst into tears. "Lord," he sobbed, "what sort of a life have we Jews got? Our enemies destroyed our most sacred temple and drove us from the Holy Land. You have dispersed us among the nations, and we know only humiliation and suffering. You have left us only one joy: your Torah, your teaching. But I have spent my whole life knitting and selling stockings. I have never learnt to read, never taken comfort in the Scriptures, but only in my box of tobacco. What sin have I committed that now I may not even have a smoke? Why have you deprived me of my tobacco box?"

Leib wept, and wept, wandering he knew not where. His steps took him into field and forest. In a glade he sank into the grass. He could not go on for grief. Suddenly he heard a loud stamping. The earth swayed beneath him like a ship on a storm-tossed sea. Leib rolled over on his back, and when he came to his senses, he did not know whether he was awake or dreaming. Standing over him was an enormous billy-goat.

The creature's legs were longer than the tallest trees, and its body was like a huge fortress wall. Its gigantic horns stretched to the sky and touched the stars, which were singing a song of praise for God and His eternal love and grace. But the most peculiar thing about the goat was its green eyes, which gazed at Leib softly and soothingly. They were not like an animal's eyes, but like those of a kindly human being.

"Why are you sad?" the goat asked the hosier. "What is troubling you?"

Summoning all his courage, Leib recounted his tale of woe. When he had finished, the goat shook its head. "Is that all?" it said. "Then I can easily help you. I shall bend my horns towards you, and you may cut off as much as you need to make a new box."

Leib got his pocket-knife ready at once. The goat bent his horns down to the ground, and the hosier cut off the tip of one of them, just enough to fit in his pocket.

The next day Leib filled his pipe with tobacco from the new box. He smoked one pipeful, then another, but the tobacco in the horn scarcely went down at all. The whole thing was quite miraculous, and what was even more wonderful was the fragrance of the tobacco. When Leib smoked it, he seemed to be inhaling the smoke of the incense in the temple of Solomon. He had never tasted anything so delicious in all his life, and he soon realized that his mind, too, was less simple than before. The more he smoked, the more he knew. The tobacco box was like a teacher, imbuing the smoke with words of wisdom, placing knowledge in each pinch of tobacco.

The rumor of Leib's strange tobacco box soon got around. Everyone wanted to know how he had come by it, and both rich and poor coveted it. The neighbors knocked on the hosier's window day and night, and the moment he stepped out of the door a crowd gathered round him to smell the smoke. But one day Leib could keep his secret no longer. He revealed not only that he had received his tobacco box from the wonderful goat with human eyes, but also the place where he had met the creature.

The next day, when Leib set off for the market-place to sell his usual three pairs of stockings, he was in for a surprise. Yankel the tanner was sitting contentedly in front of his house smoking his pipe, and as Leib approached he held up the same tobacco box as the hosier himself had. The next night the cooper, Pinchesl, also got a magic tobacco box, and after him Dov the tailor. Each morning someone new rejoiced at a gift from heaven, and the wisdom of the local Jews grew all the time.

In the meantime, Leib lived much as he had always done, except, perhaps, that he had more visitors now. As he knitted his stockings, he would speak with hasids on learned questions. He now knew more than many rabbis did, and found the solutions to many problems. But he was left with his own questions. "Where did the wondrous goat come from?" he would ask himself. "How is it possible that a tobacco box made from one of its horns radiates wisdom, as if it were a sage? And what is the meaning of the goat's human eyes?" Leib thought of the goat wherever he went, and so did all the others who had seen the extraordinary creature. The goat had changed their lives. In their tobacco boxes, too, lay the hidden power of some unknown teacher, and even the simplest among them understood the laws of God.

Several months passed. The Day of Atonement was drawing near, the great day of judgement, when the fate of every Jew is sealed in the book of God. Then the word went round that the goat had disappeared. For several nights in a row it had failed to show itself in the forest, and those who had come for a tobacco box from its horn had returned home disappointed. "Where is the goat?" they pestered Leib. "You were the first one it appeared to. Don't you know more of its secret? Can't you tell us where it has got to?"

Leib just shook his head, and was so anxious that he could scarcely breathe. That night it was a long time before he got to sleep, and when he finally did drop off he had a dream. In it he saw a small room in which an old man was standing. "Leib," he said, "tomorrow you should go into Kotsk and visit Rabbi Menachem Mendel. He will tell you where the goat is."

The next morning was the first in Leib's adult life that he did not knit stockings. The moment he woke up he set off for Kotsk, but it was an anxious journey for him. "Rabbi Menachem Mendel is a great tzaddik, a saint such as is seldom seen," he said to himself. "What if he will not receive me? And even if he does, can I tell him I have come to see him because I had a strange dream?"

Late in the afternoon Leib was knocking on the rabbi's door. The tzaddik himself opened the door, and Leib was rooted to the spot. Standing in front of him was the old man he had seen in his dream. He was wearing the same kaftan and the same *yarmulka* skullcap as in the dream. Even his voice sounded the same. "You are the last," said Rabbi Menachem Mendel, as if he had known Leib for a long time and had been told to expect him. "Come in." Bewildered, Leib went into the house, where his wonder soon increased. In a small, dim room sat a row of familiar figures. There was Yankel the tanner, Pinchesl the cooper, Dov the tailor – all those who had received tobacco boxes from the wonderful goat with the human eyes.

Leib took a seat. "What does all this mean?" he wondered. "Did we all have the same dream?" He was just about to ask, but no one spoke, and Leib was loath to break the silence. "Ah well," he thought, "a little patience won't come amiss." He felt carefully in his pocket for the magic tobacco box, and filled his pipe. As soon as he had lit up, Yankel did the same. Then Pinchesl began to smoke, too, followed by all the rest of the rabbi's visitors.

In a while the little room was filled with smoke. But it was no ordinary smoke. When the fragrance of all the miraculous tobacco boxes was combined, the room became redolent with the perfume of Paradise itself. But now Leib and those who sat with him did not merely see into the mysteries of the holy books, as they had before. The knowledge of their unknown teacher revealed to them a new experience – that of heaven itself. Leib had long since forgotten why he came to see Rabbi Menachem Mendel; he did not even know whether it was day or night. Hours drifted by, but no one spoke a word.

Then suddenly, the wonderful smoke dispersed a little. The magic passed, and Menachem Mendel spoke quietly: "People ask you to tell them where the goat is. They think that since you have received tobacco boxes from its horn, they will get them too. But you, who know more than other mortals, should know the truth. The goat will give no more boxes to anyone. His horns, which dispensed wisdom and happiness, no longer reach up to the heavens. There is not the smallest piece of them left."

Leib gazed into the rabbi's face. Suddenly he saw that the eyes were the same as those of the remarkable animal, that the mysterious goat, the invisible teacher, who had comforted the downcast and taught the unlearned, had been the tzaddik himself.

"Rabbi," sighed Leib, and all the others spoke at the same instant. They all leapt up and hurried towards the rabbi. But Menachem Mendel took a step backwards. "I have given you all I could," he said, in a weary voice. "Go now, and tell others what you have learnt from me." Silently, he shook hands with them all, and when his visitors had gone, he shut himself up in his room. From that day on no one ever spoke to Rabbi Menachem Mendel. He lived quite alone, and died, too, in solitude.

Faivl Lost
and Found

In the Polish town of Pszisch there once lived a hasid called Faivl. He was a hasid good and proper: he wore only a tattered kaftan smelling of tobacco and onions, and on his head a *streiml*, a fur cap with sable tails hanging from it. His temples were adorned with long, meticulously curled side-whiskers. There were none in the whole town to compare with them, and Faivl took as much pride in his whiskers as a bride in her wedding-gown. But he was prouder still of his learning. He would sit in the house of study, the *beit hamidresh*, in Pszisch all day long, and at night-time, too, he could be seen warming his seat on the bench there. The rest of the hasids gathered in the beit hamidresh after work: the second-hand dealer when he had bought and sold his goods, the cobbler when he had sewn his shoes, the carter when he had delivered his load. Their fingers were hardened and blackened with daily toil, while Faivl's were as soft and white as feathers, having never handled anything rougher than the leaves of learned books; indeed Faivl behaved as though he had written the books himself.

In short, Faivl was too conceited for words, but actually he mixed everything up. What he read in the morning he had forgotten by evening, and what he learned at night he put out of his head in his sleep. Though he contemplated why what is so is so and what is not so is not, his reasoning made him no more reasonable than before. His studies were all at sixes and sevens, and he forgot one book on account of the next. If Faivl had not turned his nose up at the hasids of Pszisch and had paid attention during their learned discussions, he would have realized that his head was quite empty. But Faivl was not interested in anyone else's company. He would sit apart from the others and not speak a word to anyone. He was convinced that he understood the Torah better than anyone, and his admiration for his own learning grew day by day.

Weeks went by like that, and months and years. Faivl was pleased with being such a *hochem*, a wise man, but his happiness was not complete. He had one worry, and it was no mean one. Whenever he woke up in the morning and wanted to set off for the house of study, he could not find his clothes. He never knew where he had put his kaftan or his streiml; if he found his left shoe, the right one was missing, and if he happened to find both of them neither had any laces in it. "Ah, well," Faivl assured himself, "such is the fate of men of great learning. Their minds are lifted up to heaven, and they have no thought for the earthly world."

But one day all the forces of Satan must have ganged up on Faivl. First he couldn't find his glasses, and when at long last he managed to feel them out, his whole room was upside down. Eiderdowns and pots and pans and everything else in it had ended up in one great pile. It was midday before Faivl succeeded in fishing out his clothes, and the thought of how many hours in the beit hamidresh he had missed made his heart ache. "I can't go on like this," he said to himself. "Tonight I shall make a list of what is where and put it under my pillow, then in the morning I shan't have to look for anything."

The moment Faivl got back from the beit hamidresh he did as he had resolved. "The kaftan is on the chair," he wrote in large letters, "the streiml is on the table, both shoes are under the bed, and I am in the bed." Adding an emphatic full stop, he pushed the piece of paper under his pillow and went to sleep with a glow of satisfaction.

At dawn Faivl awoke happily. Drawing out the piece of paper from beneath his pillow, he leapt to his feet. "The kaftan is on the chair," he read. So he took his kaftan from the chair, put it on, and went on reading. "The streiml is on the table." That, too, he found without any trouble, as he did the shoes beneath the bed. "I am in the bed," he read at the end of the note. He peered beneath the eiderdown, and turned quite pale: the bed was empty.

"There is no hasid in Pszisch who has studied more than I," thought Faivl, horrified, "therefore I am the most learned. If it is written in my own hand where I left everything last night, and since I found everything else where it was supposed to be, then that is quite clear. The word of the wise is like the law. But I did not find myself, and that means..." Faivl swallowed with difficulty, then gulped in a voice filled with horror: "There is no doubt about it — I have vanished in the night!"

The hasids of Pszisch did not see Faivl in the house of study that morning, nor was there any sign of him that afternoon or evening, or during the following days. No one had any idea what had happened to him, and no one knew he had set out into the world to look for himself.

Faivl wandered through field and forest, from one strange village to another, wherever his steps took him. But it was not long before his stomach began to rumble, and the hungrier he got, the more anxious he grew. "What if no one invites me to his table?" he worried. "At home my wife looked after me, but here in the open countryside I shall die without food. If I die, then I shall never find myself again. And if I don't find myself, how can I appear before the heavenly council of judgement? What is someone who has lost himself to do in heaven?"

As Faivl was thus pondering his plight, he saw in front of him a tall, beautiful house with a large garden. "This is surely the home of some rich man," he thought. "He wants for nothing, and I can scarcely walk I am so hungry. I hope to heaven I will find food and shelter here."

He went up to the door and knocked. When a servant opened the door, Faivl told him he would like a bed for the night and a little food, and the servant led him to his master. "You are in luck," the rich man told Faivl. "You have arrived just at the right time; if you wish, you may earn your bed and board."

"What am I to do?" Faivl asked.

The rich man motioned to his visitor to follow him, and led the way to the stables. A fine white horse was stamping about beside its trough. "I bought this splendid horse only today," the rich man explained. "It is so valuable that I have had a new stable with a strong door built for it, but I require a guard also. Would you like the job?"

Faivl was delighted. "Guarding horses is easy enough," he thought. "I shall only sit and think how I am to find myself, and I shall eat and sleep well." So he accepted the rich man's offer without hesitation. He had a good meal and, as soon as darkness fell, wrapped himself up in a thick blanket and went and sat in front of the stables.

While Faivl was looking after the precious white horse, the rich man was unable to sleep. He was afraid someone would steal the animal, and he tossed and turned all night, until, early the next morning, he could contain his anxiety no longer, and got up to see for himself. He dressed and, quietly, just like a thief, crept out to see if his horse was safe. He managed to enter and leave the stable without Faivl's even noticing.

"Are you asleep, or what?" he asked, shaking Faivl.

"How could I sleep?" asked Faivl. "I am thinking."

"About what?"

"About a question of some difficulty," replied Faivl, weighing his words. "If a nail is driven into a piece of wood, what happens to the wood from where the hole is?"

The rich man was surprised. "You think about some strange things," he said, "but I took you on to look after my horse, not to sit here philosophizing. Mind you remember that!"

Faivl promised to be more alert, and the next night he guarded the valuable horse again. Once again the rich man was unable to sleep for fear someone should take his horse, and he stole unnoticed into the stable. When Faivl again made no attempt to stop him, he turned on his guard angrily: "Yesterday I told you to pay more attention, and tonight you are guarding no better than before!"

"I cannot help it," Faivl told him. "I am the sort of person who must constantly think about something. I was just wondering where the wax goes when a candle burns."

His master warned him: "I should rather you thought about my horse and not about trivialities. I am telling you for the last time: if I find once more that you are not doing your duty, I shall get rid of you even if it means your dying of hunger!"

When the evening of the third day came, Faivl ate and drank his fill and went to the stables as before to keep watch over the horse. As soon as he had taken his place, he became engrossed in thought. He pondered how best to find himself, and was drawn towards other thoughts, and before he knew it dawn was breaking. Suddenly his irate master was shaking him. "What are you doing?" he thundered, ruddy with anger. "The horse is gone!"

Faivl nodded his head, unperturbed. "I know," he said, deliberately. "I was just wondering where it had got to, when the stable is still standing, the door is as strong as ever, and I am sitting in front of it."

The rich man hurled himself at Faivl, beating him ferociously and pulling him by the side-whiskers he was so proud of; as he did so he cursed all dabblers, clowns and pedants, until his shouts woke the whole household.

Blow after blow rained down upon Faivl. His body burned like fire, and it suddenly occurred to him: "If I can feel pain in my back, it must be my back. And where my back is, I must be too. I have found myself!" With a cry of joy, Faivl extricated himself from his angry master's grip, and hurried home as fast as his legs could carry him.

From that time onwards Faivl became a different man altogether. Until he went out into the world, he scarcely took any notice of the other hasids, but his beating changed him. He realized that there is a world other than the one he carried around in his own head, and stopped supposing he was the cleverest person in the world. He went out to work like the other hasids, and never studied alone any more, but always with others. His memory ceased to be like a sieve; the wisdom of the books was opened up to him, and Faivl would have sworn he could sometimes hear in the rustling of their pages the wings of the angels who watch over those pupils best beloved of heaven. Faivl's learning grew day by day, and he no longer immersed himself in mere sophistry, so that he never had to go looking for himself again.

Spilt
Soup

The town of Liszensk has stood in the middle of Poland since time immemorial, and many, many years ago a certain Rabbi Elimelech lived there. Elimelech was a tzaddik. His soul ascended to heaven while he was still alive so that he might converse with the celestial orders; it was so pure and clear that everything which had happened since the Creation was reflected in it. Rabbi Elimelech knew what father Abraham had looked like, and he remembered Moses with his wonderful staff, and the great King Solomon.

There are those learned men who wrap themselves up in their knowledge like a coat. They are silent, and warm themselves with their own learning, while they let others freeze out in the cold. But Elimelech was not a rabbi in a fur coat. He shared the warmth of his heart with all who needed it, so that his hasids warmed themselves around their tzaddik as if they were in a pleasantly heated room. The best time of all was after lunch on the Sabbath. They would listen to the wise words of Elimelech, at the same time laughing and rejoicing together, enjoying each other's happiness.

They lived like that for many contented years, until one autumn day sad news reached Liszensk. In the distant capital, the chancellor, who was no friend of the Jews, had made up his mind that he would make all Jewish boys join the army. He had drawn up a law to that effect and placed it in a golden document case, and all that was needed now was the emperor's signature.

Anxiety spread among the Jews of the realm. "If our boys become soldiers, they will not be able to learn the holy Torah," they said. "They will not be able to observe the customs of their ancestors; they will be lost in the world like a drop of water in the sea. They will march instead of praying, and will have to work on the Sabbath and on holidays." Gloom descended on all Jewish households, and in Liszensk, too, the Jews mused on the hard fate of their nation in exile, and on the trials they had to suffer.

The day was approaching when the emperor was to give his assent to the new law. Jews throughout the land collected money to try to dissuade their ruler, and sent secret messengers to the imperial palace, but all their efforts were fruitless. The wicked chancellor would not let anybody near the emperor, turned down all the money that was offered, and, to add insult to injury, announced that the emperor would put his signature to the law on the Sabbath.

On the holy day in question it seemed in the synagogue in Liszensk as if the local hasids must be recalling the destruction of the temple at Jerusalem. They were dressed in white robes, and they prayed, wept and lamented. When the service was over, it was time for Rabbi Elimelech's wife to bring the Sabbath lunch to the table. Many of the rabbi's pupils had gathered in his house, among them the tzaddik's favorites, Jacob Yitzhak, who had the gift of Elimelech's all-seeing vision, Abraham Joshua, who had learnt how to judge as fairly as the rabbi himself, and Israel of Kosnice, who could pray like his teacher. But in the place of honor at the rabbi's right hand sat Mendel. Only he had received the strength of the tzaddik's soul, and he had been chosen as his successor.

Rabbi's wife Gitl began to pour the soup. What a cook she was! Whether the soup was thick or thin, it always had the aroma of Paradise, for the angels added a little heavenly

seasoning to it. Such were the celestial merits of Gitl, and the rabbi always swallowed her food in just as reverent a manner as if he had sat not beneath a thatched roof, but at the table of the just in Paradise. But this time he did not even touch his soup. He stared silently into the full plate; then suddenly, before anyone knew what was happening, he had flung it onto the tablecloth.

The rabbi's pupils did not know what to think. They looked at each other uncomprehendingly; only Mendel fixed his big, dark eyes on the tzaddik. "Rabbi," he whispered, "is it not enough that we must serve in the army? Are you saying they will throw us in prison, too?"

The rabbi shook his head, "Do not be afraid, Mendel," he said. "The important thing is to have enough soup."

By now Jacob Yitzhak, Abraham Joshua and Israel of Kosnice had grown quite uneasy. "What on earth are the rabbi and Mendel talking about?" they thought. "Is it possible the idea of the cruel fate which has befallen the Jews has affected their minds?"

But they had scarcely had time to collect their thoughts when the rabbi's wife Gitl poured her husband another plate of soup. And again the rabbi did not eat it, only stared into the steaming plate as if he were looking for something there, then suddenly overturned it as before. The soup dripped from the tablecloth onto the floor, and there was a heavy silence. Mendel turned quite pale, while the rest of the pupils hung their heads. Their hearts were gripped with fear for their beloved rabbi, and they inwardly tried to exorcize all evil spirits and unclean powers. But Rabbi Elimelech behaved as if nothing had happened. He calmly motioned to his wife to pour him a third plate of soup. Gitl hadn't got much left, and she had to turn the dish upside down, but she managed to fill his plate. The tzaddik breathed heavily, leaving his spoon where it lay. Then he made a sudden movement and, placing his hand on the edge of the plate, turned it over in a measured fashion. Elimelech's face began to beam, and Mendel embraced the rabbi.

The pupils leapt up from their seats and pressed towards the door in panic, as if the depths of Hell were opening up beneath them. "The rabbi has gone mad! The rabbi has gone mad!" they cried. They blundered about the town, tearfully spreading the sad news that one misfortune had led to another, that Rabbi Elimelech had gone off his head.

But it was not only in Liszensk that alarm and despondency prevailed. Far away in the imperial palace there was a state of panic as if a fire had just broken out. At the very moment when Gitl had poured her husband's first plate of soup, the emperor had been about to put his signature to the law that the Jews must serve in the army. The chancellor took the fateful law out of its golden case, the emperor dipped his golden quill into his golden inkpot, and at that moment, no one knew why, the inkpot was overturned. In an instant the paper was black with ink, and the emperor motioned impatiently to the chancellor to give him another sheet of paper with the same text. Once more he dipped the end of his golden quill into the golden inkpot and bent over the parchment, but before he had managed to sign his imperial assent, the inkpot was overturned again. Once more the words were obliterated by the ink, and the emperor lost his temper. He stamped his feet and shouted, and swung out at everyone within reach. The chancellor tried to give the monarch a third copy to sign, but that ended badly too. The emperor tore the law to shreds, raving and shouting abuse, and declared that he would never sign that document, so that in the end the chancellor was grateful not to end up in prison.

A few days later a messenger from the imperial city arrived in the province of Liszensk. He informed the astonished hasids that the Jews need not enter the army, and with eyes raised skywards told of the incredible events which had accompanied the attempted signing of the infamous law.

The Jews began to rejoice. They celebrated their unexpected reprieve, sang and made merry. Suddenly Elimelech's pupils realized why it was the emperor had been unable to sign the law, and just then the whole town gathered around the rabbi's house. His pupils begged his forgiveness, weeping with shame and joy. But the tzaddik only smiled. "No matter," he said. "Mendel was with me in spirit, so I was not afraid of the emperor."

From then on the fame of Rabbi Elimelech increased still further. Soon the rumor spread throughout the realm that the emperor's footman had bumped into the table as the monarch was signing the law, so that the inkpot had twice been overturned; the hasids of the Liszensk province swore they had witnesses to prove it. Why should they not do so much for their miracle-working tzaddik? His secret was their secret, and if the emperor had learnt it, who knows what might have become of Rabbi Elimelech?

The Boiled Chicken

Many years ago in Berdichev in the Ukraine, seat of the famous Rabbi Levi Yitzhak, lived a hasid called Herschel. He was quite alone in the world, and his only companion was poverty. But Herschel did not mind. "What is money for?" he would say, repeating the words of the rabbi of Berdichev. "For the rich to give, and the poor to receive." And since Herschel had none to give, he wandered from place to place, asking good folk for a piece of bread and a little straw to sleep on.

One day at noon, Herschel stopped at an inn which belonged to a very mean woman. If she could, she would have charged her guests for the air they breathed, and she would have liked to make soup from plain water. Before she placed on the table a bowl of soup from dog's-tail-grass seeds, she would stop three times to pour a little back into the pan; but her prices were high, just the same. She knew well enough that there was not another inn for miles around, and that she would not lose her customers no matter how deep they had to delve into their pockets.

When Herschel appeared in the doorway, the innkeeper frowned. She was hoping to see a rich merchant from a distant city who was due to pass by that day, and here instead was a pauper. It was pouring with rain outside, and the bedraggled Herschel looked even more down-at-heel than usual. His tattered hide coat was so small that he could not even fasten it; his trousers were tied up with string, and his toes were sticking out of his boots.

"What do you want?" the innkeeper asked, gruffly.

"What should I want?" Herschel replied. "My wife is dead, my children too, and there is no one to look after me. Only give me a little food, I beg you, and let me stay under your roof until I dry out a little."

The innkeeper began to think furiously: "If I give this beggar food, I shall lose money. But if I only let him sit by the stove, it will cost me nothing, and no one can say I am inhospitable." So she said to Herschel: "I cannot give you anything to eat. I have sold everything, and it will be impossible to buy more food until tomorrow. But you may dry yourself if you wish. Sit down on the bench by the stove — but as soon as the rain stops, you must be on your way!"

So Herschel took off his coat and his boots and made himself comfortable near the stove. He leaned back and stretched out his legs — and suddenly became aware of the smell of boiled chicken. "What can that be?" he thought. "Am I imagining things in my hunger?" He took a good look around him, and saw a large pot standing on the stove. Its lid was dancing up and down, and every so often the innkeeper would peep into it with satisfaction.

"What's that you are cooking?" Herschel asked. "It smells like chicken."

"What are you thinking of?" the innkeeper replied. "I told you I have nothing to eat. I am boiling my washing in the pot — sometimes it smells like chicken."

But Herschel was not to be put off so easily. He could sniff out boiled chicken a mile away, and when he thought of the drumsticks, wings and soft breast, his mouth began to water. He was so hungry he felt as if there was an iron hoop around his stomach, and he could not even look at the pan containing such a delicacy. He thought he had better close his eyes, but he couldn't escape the smell. He wondered if it might not have been better to stay out in the rain, and as he sat there motionless the innkeeper thought he had gone to sleep. "I'll go and take a nap, too," she said to herself. "Anyway, no one is likely to come in this pouring rain, and at least I shall have a rest before the rich merchant comes." She took a last prod at the elegant chicken and took the pot off the stove.

The moment the door closed behind the innkeeper, Herschel opened his eyes. He looked around and, seeing he was alone in the kitchen, leapt to his feet. He grabbed the pot containing the chicken, and began eating. He ate the legs and the breast, stripped the wings and the neck, and didn't leave even a scrap of skin. In a while all that was left in the pot was chicken broth and a little pile of bones. Then Herschel fished a dirty old shirt out of his linen bag. He dropped it into the pot, replaced the lid, and stood the pot as it had been before.

An hour later the innkeeper woke up. It had stopped raining outside, so she hurried over to Herschel to send him on his way. But Herschel was in no mood to travel. After his excellent meal he slept like a log, and the innkeeper had to give him a good shaking to wake him up. At that moment the door opened, and the long-awaited guest came in with his manservant and coachman. All three of them sat down at the table.

"Give us the best you have," the merchant told the innkeeper. "I have money enough — just as long as it is something tasty."

"I have cooked you a chicken," the innkeeper replied, "such as you have never tasted in your life before." All smiles, she brought the pot from the stove and set it down on the table. "Help yourselves," she invited them.

The merchant did not wait to be asked twice. Grabbing a fork, he stuck it into the pot, and instead of a chicken fished out a soiled and soppy shirt, from which a couple of chicken bones slid back into the broth.

The innkeeper nearly fainted. "It must have been him!" she shrieked, pointing at Herschel, who was just drawing on his ventilated boots. "He must have eaten it!"

Herschel took no notice of her. "Good sir," he said, turning to the merchant. "Judge for yourself whether I am guilty. I asked this woman for a little food, but she refused.

She said she had nothing, and that she was boiling washing in the pot. Was there anything wrong with my adding a shirt to it?"

The merchant rose to his feet. He was not only a rich man, but a god-fearing one, too, and always saw to it that the poor were looked after. When he heard how Herschel had tricked the miserly innkeeper, he laughed merrily. "A good thing I didn't eat in this house," he said. "A skinflint like her doesn't deserve a blessing after a meal. She brought her loss upon herself, and now at least she will remember that one must help the poor."

The innkeeper was beside herself with rage. She had lost both her chicken and her profit. But Herschel was in a joyful mood. He had eaten a good meal, and the merchant took him a good way in his carriage, and gave him a little money when they parted.

The Trees and Iron

When iron was created, all the trees were sad. "What a fate," sighed the forests, groves and gardens, "God has sent a cruel enemy upon us. The day will come when men will make axes out of iron, and chop us all down."

Iron heard the trees lamenting, and replied: "You have nothing to fear. Your fate is in your own hands. As long as you do not betray your own kind by allowing yourselves to be used as hafts, nothing can happen to you. But if you are not united, and if you join forces with me, then the axe will indeed bring you death."

Gold
and Iron

One day gold set out into the world. It walked, and walked, until it arrived at a place where it could hear a terrible sighing and wailing. "What can that be?" said gold to itself. It went closer and saw a forge, where a blacksmith was striking a piece of hot iron with a great hammer. At each blow the iron groaned, and there was no end to its suffering.

"Why do you lament so?" gold asked the iron. "All metals are beaten — even I, gold, have the same fate. Men long for me, but I am struck just as you are."

"How can you compare our fates?" sighed iron bitterly. "I am a metal, as you are, it is true, but there is a difference between us. You are beaten by iron, not gold, and it is quite usual to suffer at the hands of strangers. But I am struck by my own brother, and that is a pain worse than any other."

THE EIGHTH
LIGHT

Chelm –
the Jewish Gotham

The Building
of Chelm

When God made the world, He also made the souls of all men. He placed the souls of the wise in one sack and the souls of fools in another, and commanded one of the angels to distribute them throughout the earth. The angel took the sacks, and off he went. He flew over all the lands of the earth, sprinkling a handful of wise souls and a handful of foolish ones everywhere he went, so that equal numbers of wise and foolish people were born. But in a certain place the angel grew careless; as he was flying over a high mountain, he got one of the sacks caught up in the crown of a tree, and as he tugged it free he tore a big hole in the sack. All the remaining wise souls fell out onto the ground. So it was that all the people who were born there were to be clever, sharp-witted and ingenious — in short the wisest of the wise. They became famous throughout Poland, and their great deeds swelled the renown of their city, which they themselves named Chelm.

Once upon a time the Chelmites decided to build themselves some proper houses. There was no lack of timber. The mountain on which the careless angel had dropped the souls of their ancestors was thickly overgrown with trees, and the Chelmites selected the stoutest of them. What trunks they had! They were so large and heavy that it was as much as ten strong men could do to lift them. The Chelmites carried timber for a month, but they still had more of it up on the mountain than down below.

As they were carrying down a huge trunk, a Jew from Lithuania happened to pass by. "Why waste so much effort?" he asked the Chelmites. "If you were to give the trees a good shove, they would come rolling down the hill of their own accord, and you would save yourself all that work!"

The Chelmites could have kicked themselves. They ran off to inform the elders, who listened with mouths open wide. "We shall consider the foreigner's advice," they said, nodding their heads gravely. "A matter such as this requires consideration!"

So the wisest of the Chelmites sat in council for seven days and seven nights. In the morning they thought about the matter, in the afternoon they weighed up the pros and cons, and in the evening they turned it over in their minds before sleeping on it. On the eighth day they proclaimed that the Lithuanian Jew was right. "From now on we shall roll the logs down from the mountain," they decided. "Why should we carry them on our shoulders for nothing?" They wrote a long entry in the community book on the subject, and all the elders confirmed in writing that not only the inhabitants of Chelm, but also the Jews of Lithuania, had their heads screwed on the right way.

The next day the Chelmites set off with great pomp and circumstance up the mountain. Music played as if a rabbi's son were getting married; there was even more merriment than on Simhat Torah, the feast of Rejoicing in the Law. The strongest of the men took the tree-trunks they had so laboriously brought down from the mountain, hoisted them onto their shoulders, and with eyes popping from exertion began to carry them back up again. When they got there, they gave the logs a light push with their feet, and watched with smiles of happiness as they went rolling and bumping down the hill, coming to rest at last far below.

When the Chelmites had thus got together enough wood to build their houses, they took up their saws, axes, hammers and planes. Soon the whole town was filled with

a mighty sawing and banging. Houses appeared one after another, as if they were growing out of the ground; it was not long before the valley at the foot of the mountain was filled with streets. But the Chelmites were not content to put up just any old sort of buildings. Not a wall was raised until they had measured themselves from head to foot, so that their houses were neither too high nor too low. They fitted the Chelmites like well-tailored waistcoats, and any visitor could see at once who were the tall ones and who the small ones.

The day came when all the Chelmites had a roof over their heads. They congratulated themselves on how much timber they had saved by measuring the houses to fit the people, and they swaggered importantly from one end of the town to the other. Ducks waddled along the streets among the dignified elders, and goats bleated at the windows. The Chelmites surveyed their work proudly, until all of a sudden a cry of horror went up. They had forgotten to build a synagogue!

If the whole of Chelm had lain in ashes, it would not have been a greater blow to its inhabitants. The elders of the community met that very evening, and before the cock crew they had announced their decision: the foundations of the synagogue must be laid in the centre of the town.

The Chelmites set to work right away. They dug the foundations in the town square and felled some particularly massive trees up on the mountain; these they sent rolling down the hill with a single shove. More men were already waiting at the bottom. Ten of them heaved each trunk onto their shoulders, and they set off towards the site of the synagogue like a troop of well-drilled soldiers. But they had not gone far when they came up against an unexpected obstacle. The streets of Chelm were narrow, and their broad load was unable to pass between the first of the houses. Try as they might, the men could not get into the street, and they did not come an inch nearer to the foundations of the synagogue.

What were the Chelmites to do? They informed the elders of the community, whose deliberations took seven days and seven nights. They started weighing up the pros and cons first thing in the morning, so that they could spend all afternoon thinking about the matter, before brooding about it in the quiet of the evening. Then they decreed: "The synagogue must be built! All houses which are in the way are to be removed at once!"

The Chelmites rejoiced at the wisdom of their leaders. They knocked down one half of the city, carried the logs to the place the synagogue was to be built, and then rebuilt the houses.

When everyone in Chelm had his own house, and all the people of Chelm had their own synagogue, the only thing they still had to put up was a *mikveh*, a bath-house for the citizens to wash themselves in before the Sabbath and feast days. They soon found a site for it, by the stream on the edge of the town, and the building of it didn't take them long, either. They built a mikveh which was just as it ought to be, with walls, a roof and windows. The only thing missing was the benches inside.

A dispute arose among the Chelmites. "The benches must not be planed," some said. "If the wood is smooth people will slip on it, and there will be an accident."

"If the benches are not planed, we shall be full of splinters," objected others.

The argument was a major one, and it had to be decided by the elders of the community. They sat and racked their brains for seven days and nights. Since the question was a particularly thorny one, they turned it over in their minds in the morning and did their thinking about it in the afternoon, leaving the weighing of pros and cons until evening. In the end they decided: "There is something in what both sides say. Therefore the planks for the benches will be planed on one side and rough on the other. But so that no one can slip on them, the smooth side shall be underneath."

From then on, life was kind to the Chelmites. Nothing troubled them, and they were pleased with their wisdom, and praised each other's learning. But it was not long before they ran short of space in the town. There were more and more children, but the same number of houses as always, so the elders of Chelm were faced with a serious decision: Where were they to build new houses, when the town was right up against the mountain as it was, and there was no room at all left in the valley?

They held a council for seven days and seven nights, and then continued for a further seven days and nights. They weighed the pros and cons, thought about it and turned it over in their minds morning, noon and night, and stroked their grey beards thoughtfully until all the whiskers fell out of them. Finally, they were able to announce: "The mountain will have to be pushed back a little, so that there will be room for everyone."

The day after this momentous decision was reached the whole city gathered at the foot of the mountain. The wisest Chelmite of all gave the signal, and hundreds of pairs of hands were placed against the rock. The Chelmites pushed for all they were worth, until the sweat began to drip from them. So the men took off their coats, laid them down by the path, and heaved at the mountain once more.

Just then three travelers came passing by. While the Chelmites were pitting their strength against the mountain, the three took their coats and quietly made off with them. The citizens did not notice anything. They were steaming with sweat, and their grunting and wheezing could be heard for miles around. But in a while they grew tired, and sat down to take a rest. They looked in astonished disbelief at the flattened grass where their coats had lain a moment before, and suddenly began to shout with glee: "See how far we have pushed the mountain! Why, our coats are quite out of sight!"

The Chelmites leaned against the mountain once again. This time they shoved with even greater vigor, dreaming of how their city of the wise might grow, and grow, until it filled the whole world.

The Curious Cobbler

The world is a big place, and there are quite a few Jews in it, but you'd be hard put to find another bunch of clowns like those that lived in the Polish town of Chelm. One of them was Geitzel the cobbler, who lived in a little house with his wife and six children. He was known as curious Geitzel. Whether he was on his way to get some leather, or taking a pair of shoes to a customer, he would take in everything that was going on around him. He turned his head hither and thither, until it was a wonder he didn't twist it off altogether, and not the slightest rustle or the merest whisper escaped his notice. He was here, there and everywhere. It was a mystery how he ever found time to make shoes at all.

One Sabbath's eve, Geitzel set off for the *mikveh*, or baths, to wash all the dirt from his body in preparation for the day of rest. In the mikveh were a couple of visiting merchants, who laughed and talked as they bathed. When they began to speak about Warsaw, Geitzel really pricked up his ears. They said it was a great and beautiful city, and described the houses and the people who walked its streets. They said it was a miracle to behold.

That evening, when Geitzel returned from the synagogue, he was ill at ease. Even the appetizing smell of the Sabbath fish and the freshly baked *hallah* failed to raise his spirits. He went about like a man in a dream, not saying a word, not even singing the Sabbath songs. The moment the children fell asleep, he said to his wife: "Frodl, I have made up my mind. As soon as the Sabbath is over, I will set out for Warsaw."

Now, Geitzel's wife could hardly have been more taken aback if the house had come tumbling down about her ears. "What will you do there?" she asked tearfully. "Isn't Chelm good enough for you any more?" and she wept and wailed, begged him and cajoled him; but to no avail. Geitzel was not to be dissuaded. He explained that Warsaw was one of the wonders of the world, something he had to see; he promised to bring them presents, and swore by all the angels, both good and evil, that he would return soon.

In the end, with a heavy heart, Frodl agreed to let him go. The next day, as soon as the first stars appeared and the evening prayers brought the Sabbath to a close, she prepared Geitzel some food for his journey. He wrapped it in a bundle and, like a good Jew, added his phylacteries and his prayer book; then, early in the morning, while everyone was still fast asleep, he left his native Chelm.

Geitzel walked and walked, until round about midday he began to feel both tired and hungry. He sat down by the roadside at the edge of a forest, and ate some barley-meal pancakes with onions and had a drink of spring-water. And as he sat there, he began to make himself more and more comfortable. He took off his boots and loosened his belt. "Ah, well," he said to himself, "Warsaw is not going to run away. I'll have a little sleep — what difference does it make if I see Warsaw an hour sooner or later?" So he placed his bundle under his head, stretched himself out, and then — up he jumped with a start! What if he were to forget in his sleep which direction he was traveling in, and instead of going on to Warsaw should set off back to Chelm? He pondered how he might get over this awkward problem, toying with first one solution, then another, until at last he had a splendid idea. He grabbed hold of his boots, and laid them down on the road with the toes pointing towards Warsaw and the heels towards Chelm. "Now there is no danger of making a mistake," he thought with satisfaction. "Warsaw in the direction of the toes, Chelm in the direction of the heels." And before a minute had passed, Geitzel, stunned by his own wisdom, had fallen fast asleep.

As he slept, a cart laden with branches drove past. The branches were hanging down on all sides, and dragging along the ground. One of them happened to catch hold of Geitzel's boots and turned them around the other way. When the cart was gone, the toes were pointing towards Chelm and the heels towards Warsaw. Geitzel, of course, knew nothing of this. He was dreaming he had been invited to a wedding feast, and tables full of good things to eat and drink were floating before his eyes. He was awakened by cruel pangs of hunger. Puzzled, he looked around him for the tables of food; then he began to wonder what he was doing on the edge of a strange forest. But it was not long before he remembered he was on his way to Warsaw, and when he spied his boots in the roadway he gave a whoop of joy at his cleverness. Toes towards Warsaw, he repeated to himself with satisfaction, heels towards Chelm. He pulled on his boots, slung the bundle over his shoulder, and set off in the direction his toes were pointing.

What a light heart Geitzel had now! He smiled cheerily at everyone he met, and sang as he strode along. But his curiosity grew with every step he took, and his hunger, awakened by the dream, sharpened by the minute. So Geitzel quickened his pace, and he was not a bit surprised to find himself on the edge of a town before sunset. "Well now, here I am in Warsaw," he thought to himself joyfully. And with a hopeful heart he strode down the first street.

He walked backwards and forwards, up and down the town, turning his head to the right and to the left, until he suddenly became aware of the strangest thing. The more he saw of Warsaw, the more familiar it became to him; Warsaw and Chelm were as like as two peas! There were the same churned-up streets, where the mud was up to your ankles, the same houses of timber and earth, the same smell of manure, and the same clucking of hens. "What a good idea I had," thought Geitzel with satisfaction. "Who knows where I might have ended up if I had not used my boots to show the way. And Warsaw is a town worth seeing — the sort of town everyone feels at home in."

Encouraged, Geitzel made his way to the market-place. He strode past the stalls with an air of importance, peering beneath the canvas covers of the wagons and feeling

a sense of satisfaction that everything was just as it was in Chelm. "Now I know why folk are so full of praise for Warsaw," he thought. "Those who come here need have no fear of getting lost: they do not even have to ask the way. Where else might one find such a capital city as that?"

Geitzel had by now been through almost all the streets in the town. He recalled his home town of Chelm, and could find nothing in Warsaw which differed from it. Finally, full of curiosity, he made for the synagogue. He had no trouble at all in finding it — it was in exactly the same place as the one in Chelm, snuggled up against the rabbi's house in just the same way. Geitzel went inside, and almost cried out in enthusiasm for what he saw. Not only were the houses in Warsaw just like those in Chelm — even the people there were the same! The Warsaw *shammess* was the image of the one in Chelm. What was more, he straightened out the prayer shawls in just the same way, groaned in the same way as he swept the floor, polished the candlesticks for the Sabbath in the same way, and stood on tiptoe to top up the oil lamp, just as the one in Chelm did.

Geitzel slipped quietly out of the synagogue, and his feet led him of their own accord to the place where his own house would have been, if he had been in Chelm. It was just where he expected it to be, and there were even six children playing out in the yard. If Geitzel had not known that he had come to Warsaw, he would have embraced them all as his own, so well did he know their faces. Pesa, Gita and Uri were playing blindman's-buff, Channeleh and Moteleh were holding a carved wolf and Chaim, the youngest, was toddling about on his own. "The merchants were right to say that Warsaw is a miraculous place," thought Geitzel. "Whoever would have thought I should see such wonders here?"

Suddenly the door opened, and Geitzel stiffened. A woman stood there on the doorstep, giving pieces of bread to the children. Was it Frodl, or wasn't it? Geitzel couldn't make up his mind. "Of course it's not," he thought; "why, I am in Warsaw, after all, and not in Chelm!" But he stared as if transfixed, until the woman caught sight of him.

"Look, children!" she called. "Geitzel has come home! What are you waiting for? Supper is on the table."

Now that was just too much for poor Geitzel. He had by now grown used to the fact that Warsaw was like Chelm. He was no longer amazed by the resemblance between the two towns' inhabitants. But that there should be another Geitzel living in Warsaw?

Geitzel hesitated, not sure what he should do. But he was very hungry indeed, and not a little curious. Whatever would the Warsaw Geitzel say when he saw his double from Chelm? And could they really be so alike? So Geitzel pulled himself together, went inside the house, and waited. He ate the supper and found that the woman cooked a *shoulet* of barley and beans every bit as well as his wife. The children went to bed, and there was still no sign of the Warsaw Geitzel. "Very well," thought Geitzel, "I shall have to spend the night here, and tomorrow he will surely come." But the Warsaw Geitzel did not return the next day, or even in a week, or a month.

A year went by, and then another, and Geitzel was still in Warsaw. Curiosity kept him there, but he was anxious. What if someone in the town were to recognize that he was a stranger? He would be driven away in shame, and he would never find out if he really had a double. But he was afraid to go home to Chelm, as well. He had been gone a long time, and he had not bought the presents he had promised; who knew how Frodl would greet him?

What a cruel life! Geitzel was homesick for Chelm; he missed his wife and children, and to cap it all he was troubled with curiosity. He was afraid to go, and afraid to stay, and his lot grew more wearisome day by day. If he has not died, he is still suffering to this day.

The Schoolmaster's Goat

In Chelm, the city of the wise, there had lived since time immemorial a certain schoolmaster, a learned fellow and a man of the world. He taught the children the alphabet from *alef* to *tav*, and said prayers in a croaking voice. With his pupils at the *cheder* the schoolmaster was in charge, but at home his wife was the boss. He feared her more than his pupils feared the cane, and if she had told him to teach them to read from left to right instead of from right to left, he would surely have obeyed.

One morning the schoolmaster's wife woke up with pains all over. Her back ached, her feet were swollen and her throat was sore. "Husband," she gasped, "I am ill."

The schoolmaster felt his wife's nose, tapped her teeth, and saw at once that it was serious. "Dear me," he said. "What are we going to do?"

"What do you think?" his wife replied with a scowl. "You must go out and buy a goat. I have heard that goat's milk cures every ailment. It is just what I need. Hurry up, and mind you don't get cheated!"

Since he never argued with his wife, the schoolmaster set off at once to find a goat. Fortunately, he knew where to go. The neighboring town was well known for its fine, strong goats, and the teacher chose the sturdiest the dealer had to offer. Satisfied with his buy, he set off back home. He drove the goat in front of him, and rejoiced. "I got a bargain," he congratulated himself. "My wife will milk the goat and drink the milk, and she will be well again. She will not shout at me, and will make doughnuts filled with goat's cheese for the feast of Shabuoth."

As the schoolmaster marched along the road to Chelm, he saw in front of him an inn. The sun was still high in the sky, and the schoolmaster said to himself: "Who knows when I shall next enjoy such good fortune? Why shouldn't I treat myself to a tasty meal?" So he tied the goat up outside the inn, and went inside.

The schoolmaster ordered a great many dishes. He ate, drank, and, with his mouth still greasy, got talking to the landlord. He revealed that he was a respected citizen of Chelm, and told him about his sick wife and the goat he had bought for her. "My wife told me to make sure I didn't get cheated," he told the landlord with a knowing smile. "But no one can put one over on me. There isn't a better goat than mine in the whole world. She is white, and has two horns and a long beard, and when she's in the mood, she bleats."

"What's her tail like?" the innkeeper asked.

The schoolmaster was anxious to appear knowledgeable, and said: "It might have been a little longer. I wanted a goat with a long tail, but I forgot that they are only born like that in rainy years."

When the landlord heard this, he knew at once that his guest was the most Chelmian of all Chelmites. He went outside, swapped the schoolmaster's nanny-goat for a billy-goat, and returned to the inn. The schoolmaster was just getting ready to pay. He bade the landlord a cordial farewell, and before sunset was back in Chelm.

"Wife!" he called out from the yard. "I have brought you your goat. Come and milk it!"

The schoolmaster's wife went out into the yard carrying a large jug. She took one look at the creature, and began to shake with rage. "Fool!" she yelled at her husband. "It is a he-goat! Tomorrow morning you must go back to the dealer and change it!"

The schoolmaster was glad to get off so lightly. He lay awake all night thinking of what he would say to the unscrupulous dealer, and early the next morning set off once more for the neighboring town. By and by, he arrived at the familiar inn. "When things were going well," he thought to himself, "I had a good meal here; but as it turned out, my joy was ill-founded. The dealer deceived me. Perhaps if I have another meal here in my sadness all will turn out well in the end." So he tied the goat up outside the inn and went inside.

The landlord was as hospitable as he had been the day before. He brought large amounts of food, and asked about the schoolmaster's wife, and about the purpose of his journey. When he heard his guest's story, he secretly changed the he-goat for a she-goat. The schoolmaster noticed nothing. Catching hold of the rope which tied the animal, he led it off to the dealer.

"Trickster!" he shouted, "you sold me a he-goat instead of a she-goat! My wife got no milk, and she is as sick as ever!"

The dealer looked at the teacher in astonishment. "You wanted a nanny-goat, and that is what you have got," he said. "What are you complaining about?"

"Prove to me that it is a nanny-goat," demanded the teacher.

The dealer called his wife, and she filled a pot with milk from the goat. "Here is your proof," the dealer told the teacher, giving him the milk. "You can rely on my goats."

The schoolmaster smiled happily. "My wife will be pleased," he thought. "I shall bring one pot of milk, and she can have some more whenever she feels like it."

He set off with a light step to drive the goat back to Chelm, and before long he found himself standing in front of the inn. The landlord was waiting for him. He sat the school-master down at a ready-laid table, and as before got into conversation with him. He heard how his guest had got on at the goat-dealer's, and before the schoolmaster had paid his bill he managed to change the nanny-goat for a billy-goat once again. The schoolmaster suspected nothing; he arrived home glowing with satisfaction, and proudly presented his wife with the pot of milk.

"Here is your proof that the nanny-goat is a nanny-goat," he said. "Go outside and milk her!"

The schoolmaster's wife ran out into the yard, but she was back again in an instant. "You nincompoop!" she assailed him. "Since when have billy-goats given milk? The dealer has cheated you again, and made fun of you to boot!" The woman kicked up a rumpus as she had never done before, and the schoolmaster just crouched in a corner.

"I'll teach that scoundrel of a dealer!" he said to himself that night, grating his teeth. "I'll show him up in front of everyone."

At the crack of dawn the schoolmaster set out for the neighboring town for a third time. As usual, he stopped off at the inn, so when he arrived at his destination he was again leading a she-goat and not a he-goat, the innkeeper having made the swap again.

The dealer stared at the schoolmaster in surprise. "Don't tell me you're not satisfied with your goat," he said.

"How can you ask?" snapped the schoolmaster. "You know very well you gave me a he-goat when I wanted a she-goat!"

"Believe me, that animal is a nanny-goat," the dealer assured the irate schoolmaster. "If you like, I will have her milked for you."

"There's no need for that!" the teacher snapped back. "I took the milk yesterday, and still came home with a billy-goat. No, I want a rabbi to confirm that the nanny-goat is a nanny-goat and not a billy-goat!"

So the dealer and the schoolmaster found a rabbi, who duly wrote a certificate affirming that the nanny-goat was a nanny-goat, and set his seal upon it. The schoolmaster pressed the paper to his heart. "Now there is no doubt," he said to himself, with great relief. "I have bought a nanny-goat. My wife will milk it and drink its milk, and she will be cured. She will not shout at me, and she will make doughnuts filled with cheese for Shabuoth."

The schoolmaster turned on his heels and hurried homewards, whistling gaily. When he got near the inn, he hesitated. "I shall not pass this way again for a long time," he mused. "Have I to have something to eat or not?" In the end he decided to go inside. He tied his nanny-goat up in front of the inn, and when he set off for Chelm again, it was again with the billy-goat the innkeeper had left him.

Over the last three days, the schoolmaster's wife had recovered from her illness even without the goat's milk. She was waiting impatiently for her husband, and the moment she saw what he had brought, she began to berate him. She shouted and wept, saying what a fool she had married and calling all manner of retribution down upon his head.

"Why are you making such a fuss?" her husband asked her, when he had recovered a little of his courage. "I have a certificate from a rabbi to say that the nanny-goat is indeed a nanny-goat, and not a billy-goat. And if the creature refuses to be what it is, then I shall take it to court!"

The next day a memorable lawsuit was held in Chelm. The schoolmaster complained that the animal was not willing to stay what it was when he bought it, and the goat bleated whether the Chelmites spoke to it or not. After seven days and seven nights, the elders of Chelm gave judgement: "The dispute is decided in favor of the schoolmaster, since he bought a nanny-goat and not a billy-goat. But the goat is not guilty, because it seems to be the case that a nanny-goat which enters Chelm immediately turns into a billy-goat."

✡

The Chelmites
Do Business

In a small village not far from Chelm lived a carter named Simcha. He had three horses and a large cart, which he drove out whenever people needed his help. Simcha carried hay from the fields and apples to market, wedding guests to receptions and the dead to the cemetery. He was well paid for his work, so he and his wife and children did not live badly.

But one year misfortune befell the carter. One of his horses broke a leg, the other fell ill, and Simcha twice had to call the *shochet*, the Jewish butcher. The only horse he had left was old and infirm, and was not capable of pulling the cart. "What are we going to live on?" asked Simcha's wife anxiously. "Soon all our money will be spent, and we shall have to go begging."

But Simcha only smiled. "Don't you worry, Hendl," he said. "Don't forget that we live just down the road from Chelm. I shall go there and do such business with the Chelmites that we shall be better off than ever before!"

The carter groomed the last of his horses until its coat shone, and early the next morning tied it up in the market-place in Chelm, close to the synagogue. He scattered a handful of silver between the animal's hooves, and when he saw the Chelmites making their way to prayers he began to pick the money up.

The Chelmites watched Simcha curiously. In a while the *gabai*, the head of the community, asked him: "What are you doing? Did you drop your money?"

"Not at all," replied Simcha. "The horse gave me the money. Whenever he sneezes, a few pieces of silver fall from him."

The Chelmites were filled with wonder. The municipal treasury had for a long time safeguarded nothing but a few cobwebs, and the community felt it could put a horse which gave money to good use. The Chelmites began to try to persuade the carter to sell them the wonderful animal. They coaxed him, cajoled him, and finally, after long hesitation, Simcha agreed. He pocketed the hundred gold pieces the gabai had collected from the citizens, and hurried home with a feeling of satisfaction.

When the Chelmites returned from their morning prayers, they fed the horse well. It ate a great deal of oats, drank two buckets of water — and sneezed. It sneezed once, and it sneezed twice, but no money fell out, even when it had sneezed ten times.

Meanwhile, Simcha was having a feast. He had spent some of the profit he had made on good food and drink, and was making merry more than on the feast of Purim. Suddenly he saw from the window that the gabai of Chelm was coming, accompanied by the rabbi. "Hendl," he called to his wife. "Listen carefully. I am going to take one of the black cats from the yard into the forest. When the Chelmites get here, tell them I have gone to fetch firewood. Take the other black cat, tell it to fetch me, and let it go!"

Simcha hurried out of the house, just as the rabbi and the gabai of Chelm appeared at the door. "Where is your husband?" they asked Simcha's wife, blackly. "He has cheated us."

"He went to fetch firewood," Hendl replied, as her husband had instructed her. "But if you wish to speak to him, I shall send the cat for him." She let the animal out, and it was not long before Simcha returned, carrying a black cat under his arm.

The anger of the rabbi and the gabai melted away. They looked on in fascination at the messenger cat, wishing they had one like that in Chelm. They wouldn't even have to pay it, and it would carry news faster than the nimblest runner.

The visitors took hold of both Simcha's hands. "Carter," they implored him, "we will forgive you for deceiving us over the horse, and will pay you a further sum, if you will only let us have your cat."

"How could I?" Simcha cried. "Have you any idea how long it takes to train one?"

The rabbi and the gabai begged him, promised him heaven and earth, and in the end took the cat with them for 200 zloty. The moment they arrived back in Chelm, they told the cat to summon the elders of the community. The rabbi and the gabai wished to consult them over an extremely tricky question: were they to feed the cat at night, or in the morning? They waited for an hour, two hours, but no one came; even the next morning no one had come, and when the cat itself did not return, the two of them set out to look for it. They searched throughout the whole of Chelm, and discovered to their surprise that the cat had not passed their message on to the elders. They asked about the disobedient cat, but it turned out that the creature was already sunning itself back in Simcha's yard.

The Chelmites were very cross this time. They decided that the carter must return the money for both the cat and the horse, and sent five men to his house. Meanwhile, Simcha was enjoying himself, eating and drinking to his heart's content. Suddenly, he saw a wagon from Chelm approaching.

"Hendl," he said to his wife, "lie on the floor and pretend to be dead. When I tap you three times on the forehead with an egg, get up as if you had just come back to life."

Hendl had scarcely had time to lie down on the floor, when the Chelmites came bursting into the room. They were ruddy with anger, but when they saw the carter mourning his poor wife, they stopped uncertainly.

"My poor Hendl suddenly dropped down dead," wailed Simcha. "Whatever am I to do without her?" He moaned and sighed, and his eyes overflowed with tears. Suddenly he embraced his wife and cried: "Why, I shall bring her back to life!" Taking an egg, he tapped his wife on the forehead with it three times, and said: "I order you to rise from the dead!"

The moment Simcha had finished speaking, his wife stood up, alive and well, as if the Messiah, the deliverer, had come to raise the dead. The Chelmites were rooted to the spot. They forgot at once that they had come to recover the money paid for the horse and the cat, and had eyes only for the miraculous egg. "Carter," they implored him, "sell us your healing egg. We will give you three hundred zloty for it."

"I can't do that," said Simcha, with a shake of his head. "There is no doctor for miles around. Where would I be without the marvelous egg?"

"Then we will give you four hundred zloty," they shouted. "The rabbi's wife is sick, and we must help her."

Simcha continued to refuse a little while longer, then finally he let the Chelmites have the egg for 500 zloty. That day there was a great celebration in Chelm. The

inhabitants rejoiced that they were safe from the Angel of Death for ever; the happiest of all were the rabbi and his wife. True, her condition grew worse the next day, but the rabbi did not call a physician. "If the worst comes to the worst, I shall bring her back to life with the magic egg," he said to himself. But the rabbi's wife died, and the egg proved powerless to change anything.

As soon as the funeral was over the Chelmites met and took a solemn oath that the carter should not escape punishment this time. That night they stole quietly up to his house and pulled him out of bed. Then they threw him in a sack and, before he knew what was going on, tied it up securely. "For cheating us over the horse, the cat and the egg, we are going to throw you in the water," they told him. They loaded him onto a cart, and at daybreak drove him down to the river.

It was the middle of winter, and the river was frozen over. The Chelmites went off to find some axes to make a hole in the ice, leaving a single man to guard the carter. The moment Simcha was left alone with him, he began to shout furiously: "Help! I don't want to! Help! I don't want to!"

"What don't you want to?" asked his guard, curiously.

"Be the richest man in Chelm," explained the carter from his sack. "The elders of the community insist that I take money from everyone in the town, but I don't want it. So they tied me up in a sack, and if I don't take the money they will throw me in the river."

The Chelmite who was guarding Simcha untied the sack at once. "If that is the case," he said, "I will willingly take your place."

So Simcha tied his guard up in the sack, but he didn't wait for the Chelmites to come and throw it in the river. He hurried home, took his wife and children, and moved to another village. With the money he had got out of the Chelmites he built a fine house, bought a new cart and horses, and carried on his business as he had always done.

Many years later Simcha returned to Chelm. He thought no one would recognize him after all that time, but he had only to show his face in the market square, and the Chelmites came running from all sides. They grabbed him by the collar and took him to their elders.

"How did you get out of the water?" the wisest of the Chelmites asked Simcha. "Did we not throw you in the river tied up in a sack?"

"Indeed," the carter replied, "but what went on under the water is known only to myself. When I sank to the bottom, angels came swimming up and untied the sack. Then they led me into a magnificent castle full of gold and silver. They filled the sack to the brim with these, and also gave me a great many honey cakes and lots of wine from Paradise. I spent the whole day beneath the water with the angels, and in the evening they took me back to dry land. They showed me the way home, and since then I have been a rich man."

After that the Chelmites stopped worrying about the carter. They all wanted to go and fetch a treasure, and each of them insisted he was best suited to go. The wise men of the city held council for seven days and seven nights, and finally they decided to throw in the river those who had done most for Chelm: the rabbi and the gabai. When the sacks containing the two of them disappeared beneath the water, the whole town began to cheer. Since then the Chelmites have been waiting for the rabbi and the gabai to bring them a treasure, some honey cakes, and wine from Paradise. They have been waiting a long, long time. And to pass the time they tell each other tales of their wisdom, and of the fame of their city.

The Leviathan
and the Fox

When God created the world, He divided his work into seven days. First He created light, and separated day from night. Then He made the heavens, the earth and the waters, and plants sprang up on the land. On the fourth day the sun, the moon and the stars appeared in the heavens, and on the fifth day God created the first animals. It was then that the first insects and birds appeared, but along with them two monsters came into the world. The Behemoth, which was like a hippopotamus, began to roam the land, and the Leviathan made his home in the sea.

The Leviathan looked like a huge crocodile, with a long, snake-like body. It was covered in scales, but on its belly there were spines and plates as hard as iron and sharp as knives. The monster's jaws were filled with countless teeth, and it had a shining crown on its head. For the Leviathan was a great king. It ruled all the oceans and seas, and every last little fish paid homage to it. There was no scaled or finned creature mightier, and even the waters of the sea obeyed its command. God knew that if the monster were to come on dry land, the water would follow it. The seas would pour over everything, and the land would be destroyed by floods. So He attached the Leviathan to an invisible chain, by means of which He confined this sea-monster to the deeps.

The Leviathan was proud not only of its great strength, but also of its wisdom. It understood seventy tongues, and knew many secrets of life beneath the waves. But that was not enough: the giant ruler of the waters could not go ashore, because of God's chain, but it wanted at least to be cleverer than all the creatures living on land. One day the Leviathan heard that there lived on the seashore a fox, which was considered by all creatures to be the wisest of the animals. So he sent three fish to bring the fox to him. "I shall eat this fox," he said to himself. "In this way I shall acquire his wisdom, and there will no longer be any creature to match me in cleverness."

The fish swam to the shore, arriving just as the fox was going about his hunting. "Four-legged one," they called to him, "we need your help. We are looking for the fox, the cleverest creature that walks the land."

"I am the fox," replied the fox. "What do you want with me?"

"Are you really the fox?" asked the fish, overjoyed at their good luck. "If so, then listen carefully to what we have to say. We are no ordinary fish, but messengers from the Leviathan, the mighty ruler of the seas. Perhaps you have heard of him. He lives in a splendid palace beneath the waves, surrounded by luxury and attended by many courtiers. He eats the very finest food, dresses in magnificent clothes, and reads books written in a secret script. But the Leviathan has grown very old. He wishes to find a successor to his throne, but there is none whose wisdom is great enough. But now he has heard tell of you, fox, of your keen wits and your great intellect. He sent us to find you, and we beg you to return with us. We shall take you to the Leviathan, who will show you his kingdom. Then, when he dies, you will be the ruler of all the seas and of all the creatures which inhabit them."

When the fish had finished speaking, the fox paused to consider. "I have been hunting since early morning," he thought. "Now the sun is high in the sky, and I still haven't had a bite to eat. And even if I do manage to catch something, the lion, the bear or the leopard may come along. They are stronger than I am, and would drive me away from my prey, and I should continue to be hungry. But in the sea I should have plenty of everything; I should have to hunt no more. Servants would bring me my food, and sooner or later I should gain a royal crown."

So the fox said, "If the Leviathan wishes me to succeed to his throne, then I accept. But I do not know how to swim. How am I to get to his palace?"

"Nothing could be simpler," replied the largest of the fish. "Just sit on my back, and I'll take you there."

The fox did as he was told. He sat on the fish's back, and in a short while he found himself far out to sea, in the midst of huge waves. Wherever he looked, he could see nothing but water. His heart ached for a sight of blossoming trees and green grass, and he suddenly began to wonder if he had done the right thing. "What if I never again return to the shore?" he thought. "I shall be a prisoner in the ocean kingdom, and the animals of the land will think to themselves: stupid fox! How could he exchange the colors and the scents of the land for the gloom and the cold of the sea?"

The fox grew scared. He clung tightly to the fish's back, and said: "Now I am in your power. I cannot swim, and there is no escape for me. Tell me, fish: were you telling the truth? Does the Leviathan really wish to leave me his kingdom?"

And the fish replied, "There is no longer any need for me to lie to you, fox. The Leviathan, our mighty king, has determined to eat you, in order to acquire your wisdom. How could you have been so gullible? Did you really suppose that you, who walk on four legs, might rule over the kingdom of water, fins and scales?"

When the fox saw the danger he was in, he decided to use cunning to save his skin.

"Dear fish," he said. "I am not the least bit sorry that I set out on this journey with you. If the mighty Leviathan wishes to eat me in order to increase his wisdom, then that is a great honor for me. But you should have said so at once, for then I should have brought my heart along with me, since that is the seat of my wisdom."

"Your heart is not in your body?" the fish asked, looking at each other in dismay. "How can that be? Then where is it?"

"In a cave by the seashore," the fox told them. "It is the custom among us foxes to hide our heart away in a safe place when we go out hunting; we only use it when we want to think. You surely remember that I was hunting when you arrived; for this reason I have not got my heart here with me."

The fish stopped, and began considering what they should do. "How can we go before the Leviathan now?" they lamented. "If the fox has not got his heart with him, then our journey will have been in vain. What are we to do?"

"I think I might be able to advise you," said the fox, in a confidential manner. "It only depends whether or not you trust me."

"Speak!" cried the fish. "We will do as you ask, as long as the Leviathan's wishes are fulfilled."

"It is a simple matter," smiled the fox. "We must return to

the shore. I shall take my heart from the cave, and then we shall go to the Leviathan's palace."

The fish were satisfied with the fox's idea. They turned round and swam quickly to the shore. As soon as they got there, the fox jumped ashore, and began to dance and turn and leap about in great joy.

"Hurry up, fox!" called the fish. "We haven't much time. Get your heart quickly, so as not to keep the Leviathan waiting!"

But the fox took no notice. He ran from side to side, feasting his eyes on the sand, the trees, the bushes. At last, when he was tired, he stopped, looked towards the waves with the heads of the Leviathan's messengers poking out of them, and shouted, "Stupid fish! How could you believe that one can go hunting without a heart? If yours were in the right place, I should not have been able to escape you. And if I had no heart, I should never have been able to save myself!"

The fish knew they would never catch him now. They swam back to the Leviathan's palace and told their king the whole story. The Leviathan flew into a rage. He swallowed the three fish and unleashed a storm which lasted a full three days. But he never sent any more messengers to the fox. He contented himself with ruling the seas and the oceans, and the fox was never again dissatisfied with his lot, even when he was hungry.

THE NINTH
LIGHT

The Shammess,
or Caretaker

The End
of the World

At the very end of the world, far from all rivers and seas, beyond all the forests, fields, gardens and icy wastes, stands a great mountain. It is so far away that no mortal has ever seen it, and it reaches up to heaven itself. There is nothing that can compare with it for hardness, and there is not so much as a crack in its sides. It is as smooth as glass. There is only a single opening in it, right at the very peak. There, from a small hollow, gushes a clear spring.

At the other end of the world, hidden from human eyes, lies the heart of the world. For the world, too, has a heart, like every animal and every thing. The heart of the world beats, and gazes upon the clear spring. It watches the water run down from the top of the mountain, and longs for it, desires it with a great love, but cannot get any nearer to it. If the heart of the world were to make the slightest move away from where it lies, it would no longer see the mountain with the clear spring. They would be gone from its sight, and at that moment the heart would cease to beat. It would die of grief, and with it the whole world, for whoever loses his heart loses his life as well.

It is a great and mysterious magic which joins the clear spring and the heart of the world. The heart cannot live without the spring, but without the heart the spring itself would dry up. Each day at dusk it receives a gift from the heart — one day, one single day for which it can continue to flow. When that day has passed, the spring begins to sing. Only the heart of the world hears that song, and it answers the spring with a song of its own. They sing strange, magic songs, songs without words, notes, or melody, joyous or sad. The songs of the clear spring and the heart of the world are woven of strands of light. These strands rise into the sky, reaching the seventh heaven, and high above the world they spread out like a net filled with glitter and sparkle.

Day after day God's greatest angel comes to fashion the net into a new day. When it is ready he gives it to the heart of the world, and the heart gives it to the clear spring. Then the spring can gush until the next evening's twilight. But the angel of God who shapes the new day from the shining net has to be created anew each time. His head, body, arms and legs come only from the good deeds of men; but evil deeds destroy him. If people help each other, and live in peace and the fear of God, they give the angel life. But if there are always on earth more of those who kill, or steal, or deceive, the angel

will not appear. Then no one would gather the strands woven from the songs of the clear spring and the heart of the world; there would be no one to create the next day. The heart of the world could not give the spring its present; the spring would dry up, and without the spring the heart of the world would cease to beat. The birds and the four-legged creatures and mankind would breathe their last; the trees and flowers would wither, and the towns and villages disappear. The mountains would crash into the valleys, never to rise again...